Everything I Wish I Knew About Divorce – Before I Was In One!

Joy Blossom, BA(Adv)Psy, C.Hyp

BALBOA.PRESS

A DIVISION OF HAY HOUSE

Balboa Press books may be ordered through booksellers or by contacting:

Balboa Press
A Division of Hay House
1663 Liberty Drive
Bloomington, IN 47403
www.balboapress.com
844-682-1282

Because of the dynamic nature of the Internet, any web addresses or links contained in this book may have changed since publication and may no longer be valid. The views expressed in this work are solely those of the author and do not necessarily reflect the views of the publisher, and the publisher hereby disclaims any responsibility for them.

The author of this book does not dispense medical advice or prescribe the use of any technique as a form of treatment for physical, emotional, or medical problems without the advice of a physician, either directly or indirectly. The intent of the author is only to offer information of a general nature to help you in your quest for emotional and spiritual well-being. In the event you use any of the information in this book for yourself, which is your constitutional right, the author and the publisher assume no responsibility for your actions.

This book is a work of non-fiction. Unless otherwise noted, the author and the publisher make no explicit guarantees as to the accuracy of the information contained in this book and in some cases, names of people and places have been altered to protect their privacy.

Any people depicted in stock imagery provided by Getty Images are models, and such images are being used for illustrative purposes only. Certain stock imagery © Getty Images.

Print information available on the last page.

ISBN: 978-1-9822-5476-6 (sc)
ISBN: 978-1-9822-5477-3 (e)

Balboa Press rev. date: 10/15/2020

Dedication

This book is dedicated to:

My beautiful, strong, loving daughters, who continue to be my teachers and whose wisdom at times is a blessing.

All my clients, mentors and friends who have opened my eyes as they share their personal journeys and inspire me with their strength and integrity.

My boyfriend who is patient with me and helps me to be strengthened by our love relationship.

To my brother, who has inspired me by travelling this divorce journey before me and has supported me with his unwavering love in this lifetime.

For my best friend who has gone on to the other side and remains an inspiration for how I want to live my life.

Contents

CHAPTER 1

Introduction

I am Joy Blossom, I am a counsellor with over 35 years of counselling experience. I am also a Reiki Master and Sensei (Reiki Teacher), in addition I recently added the credential of Clinical Counselling Hypnotherapist (C.Hyp). Over the years I have helped countless people through hard times. I have done many Trauma, and Critical Incidence Interventions and Debriefings. I have helped coach couples and individuals about their decision to leave their marriage and supported them through this difficult process. Fortunately, I have also helped people build their relationships and rebuild relationships that have been damaged. Even so I was not prepared for the turbulence that my own marriage ending would cause.

One of my favourite definitions of Trauma is: Trying to make sense of nonsense or of something that logically does not make sense. For example: someone killing a group of people at random, such as mass shootings, does not make sense to me. Also because of the way our brains are wired our brain keeps going over data or material trying for a logical explanation and will toil trying to get something so tragic to make sense. Often with trauma, sense cannot be found, and continuing to try to make sense of the trauma can leave us feeling stuck.

This definition appears to have been me these past several years since my separation/divorce. I am somewhat like "a dog with a bone", I do not easily give up. And trying to make sense of leaving a loved one due to separation/divorce has been extremely hard for me to digest. I literally am a person that takes my stress to my stomach or "tummy" region. This may be of interest to some, if so you might care to check out the book by Louise Hay, "You Can Heal Your life".

Many of us experience stress in a variety of ways. Some get back pain, shoulder pain and headaches to name a few. Because I am body aware I can usually, through listening to my body signals, know if something is bothering me or not. I enjoy, William Glasser's Reality Therapy and I have Advanced Training in his theories. One of his students, E. Perry Good does a good job of explaining body signals in her book, "In Pursuit of Happiness." Even though I have knowledge of body systems and Psychology I am still learning and applying various theories to hopefully help me to understand what I have been going through. I see myself as a lifelong learner and in the future, I may then have other perspectives, but for now I will use to the best of my understanding the knowledge I currently have.

I have read a few books on divorce and I did not find information of managing the hurdles or etiquette of separation or divorce. This is partly what I hope to provide in this book or at least bouncing off points for further discussion. No two people are alike and there will likely not be identical solutions but hopefully a variety of problem-solving techniques will assist those in need. I do want people to have an opportunity to think about things they have yet to encounter. I appreciate learning from other's experiences. I recently learned how to Scuba

Dive and I am so glad I can learn from the experiences of others. Yet my own experiences have been unique to me, the people and environment or conditions that we have dove in to. This plus my own unique personality has impacted my experience. I hope by reading this you can gleam some understanding of your own unique situations and perhaps find some tools or insight into your particular areas of need.

The other reason I am writing this is for my own therapeutic value. I have journaled for years and find the process helps me to lay down the thoughts that swirl in my head hopefully to bring insight, healing and some clarity.

One of my favourite books for the separated/divorced person is: "Rebuilding-when your relationship ends," by Bruce Fisher, First Edition. Since his passing the Third Edition adds a new author Dr. Robert Alberti. These books use examples to help those going down the path of divorce to have sign posts of experiences that can possibly help navigate their way.

However; I was finding new turf, so to speak, that I could not find guidelines on. Surviving or navigating things like: Holidays, Funerals, Weddings and Graduations. I felt this as a need so decided to try and bring some insights and experience to share that might fill this need or give some guidance. In my experience we personally have yet to celebrate a wedding or grandchildren and perhaps there may be another book to follow....

Since being on this Separation/Divorce journey I have learned many things. I may even have some insights from how I stumbled through that may help you in my hindsight in hope of helping you prevent stumbling on your own path. I'm not sure who to credit with the saying, "Hindsight is 20/20".

After my separation/divorce I came across the book by Christiane Northrup, M.D., "The Wisdom of Menopause"-Creating Physical and Emotional Health and Healing During the Change. At the time my Doctor stated I was not in Menopause, the term used was that I was an "Intact Female", I don't like this term. I still had my menses, I prefer the word "moon time". However, reading Christiane's first chapter and how one does not produce as much oxytocin a hormone that helps women feel bonded and how changes can influence their connectedness, had me wondering if I had known this would I have been able to ward off a separation/divorce? Also, menopause can be seen as a "midlife crisis". Menopause is viewed as something like a second adolescence, where like adolescents, we tend to lean toward self-centeredness. It is described as women often have given and given and at this menopausal state women may have a sense of it being "their turn", perhaps appearing more self centered than other centered. I believe this is/was also a factor in our marriage ending.

I am also grateful to Christiane Northrup, M.D., for sharing her own personal story as I learn best through identification. She had received criticism from her colleagues for sharing her own story and this personal sharing was seen as less professional. I love it when professionals are human, I prefer someone to have faults, humanness rather than being seen as flawless. I found her more relatable and therefore was more interested in her viewpoints.

I know I will upset some people by my personal sharing. I will try not to use names, but those who are in my life will very likely be upset if they recognize themselves in my sharing. I think omitting my personal experience may risk important lessons being lost. I therefore will use personal sharing. I apologize in advance and likely have not shared my opinions with you directly out of fear. Others I have shared my viewpoints with, though I may have neglected to share that I am writing a book.

I have a deck/book of meditation cards, actually I have several, in the "TAO Oracle", by Ma Deva Padma.

Card 27, "The Corners of the Mouth", pages 144-145 impacted me. The quote in the card states:

"Consider what it would be like to live with the people and things that help you to feel good about yourself. Then consider the extent to which you are willing to go to make that a reality."

It is my belief that I had been unhappy for quite some time and this quote explains partly why I became willing to leave my marriage. I had felt energetically our home was influenced by a husband that was not happy and had not been happy for some time. I felt like a small plant that would not survive on its own in a flower pot with a larger plant. That perhaps I had grown in strength or was trying to and would have preferred to stay but was being sacrificed for the larger plant. I had my own desire to thrive and in the marital atmosphere, living with someone who was quite unsatisfied, I had managed to thrive, but it was getting harder and harder to do so.

The book I mentioned – "Rebuilding..." speaks of Leftovers. Leftovers refers to things that may influence your present from your past. For example: childhood or past relationship experiences could play a role in a current relationship or situation. I had been raised by two Alcoholic parents, that could be a whole other book. As a result, I was sensitive to my spouse's drinking and he knew this, though I am not sure he understood this. He knew of my sensitivity as when we were married I requested a dry/alcohol free wedding because my mom had died the year prior from alcoholism. He was not comfortable with this, our having a dry wedding, but went along with it. He wondered if we should state on the invite it would be a dry wedding. I told him you do not list what's for dinner on an invite. He had been to dry weddings before because of his family's religion. However; he did tell his friends that it would be a dry wedding. Imagine my surprise at our wedding when I saw his friends opening what I thought were wedding presents and it was actually their way of getting alcohol into the dance for them to drink. I didn't really mind as at least I wasn't paying for the booze as we were University Students paying for our own wedding and paying for others to drink was an expense I really didn't want to afford.

I tried over the 25 years of marriage to not comment on my spouses drinking too often, but the "leftovers" I spoke of had me more sensitive. As our daughters grew older, both our girls had commented a week apart unbeknownst to each other, in tears stating, how they hated their dad's drinking. I felt like I was watching my childhood and likely I told myself that I would not let my children suffer through what I suffered through, a parental drinking problem. As a child I had practically begged my mother to leave my father. They were not good for each other. Neither of my parents ever managed to be sober in their alcoholism and both had died young largely as a part of their drinking. In fact, my mother never admitted to having a problem even though it was quite obvious. Her body, mind and spirit deteriorated to where she was hard to recognize.

What I had not considered prior to divorce was that I could not protect my/our children from a drinking parent as in a shared custody situation I would not be around my children when they saw their father. This was difficult as I could only protect them so much. It didn't really occur to me that I would not see my children on a daily basis in separation as I had done the majority of the parenting. One blessing my children and I have noted is since my leaving their father, their father fortunately became a better father. I wish he would have done so with us staying together but this was not to be. He still drinks but this is not something I need to live with anymore. His perspective on his drinking is not similar to mine. Again, I emphasize it was I that had a difficult time with his drinking.

Others in my story may not see or agree with my opinions. It is much like various witnesses to a car accident. Each person witnessing the accident may have a different viewpoint or vantagepoint. Some of my viewpoints may be memory or my beliefs and may not be seen as facts by the other characters in this story. As they say in the 12 Step Programs: "Take what you like and leave the rest".

Chapter 1 Self Reflective Questions:

*   Are there any areas about separation or divorce that you would like more information on?

*   If so what are they?

*   Do you have any leftovers you wish you had been aware of prior to separation/divorce?
    Leftovers are things you may have learned or been influenced by from your family of origin (the Family you were raised by/ or born into). For example, the impact on you from an unhealthy parent or family member.

*   List leftovers that you are aware of from past experiences:

*   These leftovers could also come from past relationships:

*   Are there any myths or faulty beliefs that you held as true? For example, "You don't have the right to Be happy"?
    Or possibly you may have been told that you are not loveable?

*   What is your definition of trauma?

*   Have you experienced any traumas or wounds – Physical/ Mental/ or Spiritual?

CHAPTER 2

Trauma and Understanding

As I mentioned before, trauma is something that is tragic, and that you may not necessarily grasp with understanding. It's a way of coping with the unexplainable. My brother is a fire fighter. He shared a call where he and his colleagues could have been killed. A lady that had killed herself had set up lethal homemade rigged explosives to potentially kill neighbours and any rescue persons. Fortunately, the fire fighters arrived in time and dealt with a very dangerous situation where no one else was injured by disabling the devices.

My brother asked, "What would make a person do that?"

To which I replied, "don't try to overthink it, there is likely not a rational explanation for this irrational situation." A definition of trauma I told him as previously mentioned.

Several years into my divorce and though I am coping much better I still have days that my brain cannot grasp it. My heart still hurts. Time does appear to be healing as I have not cried in a few years at this point. Not that there is anything wrong with tears. Tears are healing. Tears are a release, if you were to look at tears through a microscope, toxins can be seen. In a similar grief, I lost my mother to death 35 plus years ago and I still miss her. Time appears to help with the healing and yet some days it still hurts. I compare grief to being like an ocean where some days the water (emotions) are calm and other days the waves are unexpectedly dangerous. Same with emotions at times they may be calm and other times emotions can be triggered.

Once I was with my daughters in Mexico. My eldest had forgotten her flip flops (I usually called them thongs, but my girls dislike this term as to them it refers to underwear). So, I purchased a new pair of flip flops for my daughter and they were quite expensive compared to home. I asked her to be diligent and to keep her eye on them and to not let them get out of her sight.

Later we were on the beach and it had been a relatively calm day. When all of a sudden, the waves came up high on the beach carrying the flip flops toward the ocean. I yelled to her to let them go as I figured where there was one large wave there would likely be another. She being diligent chased after the flip flops to the shore. I heard a blood curdling scream of, "Mom", as the next huge wave was about to take her and I ran and dove to reach her. I was so afraid and yet I had successfully grabbed her, (I lost my bathing top in the process, but I didn't care). The danger of the waves was confirmed when we were told the next day that a lady had broken both legs at the same beach, by a large wave. The large wave reminds me of how large grief and our emotions can be. At times grief, like the waves, can come out of the blue and throw us off.

Grief can catch us unawares, whether it be a death of a loved one or death of a marriage. People do not all grieve the same way. And recovery from grief is a process.

I thought my sharing some of my process might help

someone else. I also hoped writing this book will be cathartic. Merriam-Webster online dictionary defines catharsis as the act or process of releasing a strong emotion (such as fear) especially by expressing it in an art form.

Other women writers I admire have done this and it has helped them heal and I have benefitted from their journeys and sharing. Some authors voiced being afraid to share their own experiences for fear it would ruin their careers and I am grateful they took the risk. As already mentioned one of these ladies is Christiane Northrup, M.D. in her book, "The Wisdom of Menopause", in particular Chapter One and specifically page 23. I wonder if I had read this sooner if it would have helped me stay in the relationship and work things out? I tend to like the saying, "Things happen at the right time, space and sequence". I am not sure who to attribute this gem to. I had written this saying in a dry erase marker on my bathroom mirror for a while as a healing balm. Thank you to whoever coined this saying!

Another woman I admire for sharing her journey, her humanity and her metaphysics is Doreen virtue, PH.D. In, "The Light workers Way, Awakening your spiritual power to know and heal."

Louise L. Hay would be another woman who I am so grateful for her sharing in many of her books – the first I read was, "You Can Heal Your Life", at the back of the book she shares her own story in Chapter Sixteen. At first, I was skeptical, yet I have seen many truths in what she has taught in my own life and in the lives of clients, family and friends.

I started learning Reiki years ago and Louise Hay's

book as mentioned was reintroduced to me. My own spiritual growth did unfortunately play a part in the demise of my marriage – how sad. People are afraid of what they don't understand. And finally, I wish to thank one more woman writer though I am sure there are countless others as I am an avid reader and I am grateful even if I have not acknowledged you by name.

The author of "Simple Abundance – A Daybook of Comfort and Joy – Sarah Ban Breathnach has throughout her sharing given credit to many women and men whose wisdom has profoundly affected her even in such tasks as the daily carpool. For Sarah to acknowledge her humanness I am truly grateful.

In my life I still think /believe many "pretend" that all is good and yet they are hurting inside. In her book Sarah talks about being authentic and yet not everyone is ready for this or appreciates it. I however am one of likely countless others that thrive because others have bared their souls so that I can learn and be stronger, more human and more accepting of myself and others.

I was hired to speak with a company on "Respect in the Workplace" a few years ago. I am pleased that the material was received well. Many shared in their feedback they want to be more accountable for their own part they play in the health of the workplace. I felt this was rewarding work, potentially helping change in our world. I still am amazed that "Respect" isn't just a given that we all know about.

Because some people do not seem to automatically grant respect there is the following poem I wish to introduce. This is a poem that I keep in my office called "Anyway", it essentially states people will treat you badly and despite this the poem encourages us to do our best to be kind and to keep going anyway. This poem was introduced to me via the readings of Mother Teresa, from a sign on the wall of Shishu Bhavan, the children's home in Calcutta. The poem, 'Anyway', written by Dr. Kent M. Keith, his book is titled "Anyway: The Paradoxical Commandments: Finding Personal Meaning in a Crazy World." :

Anyway

People are unreasonable, illogical and self-centred,
LOVE THEM ANYWAY
If you do good, people will accuse you
of selfish, ulterior motives,
DO GOOD ANYWAY
If you are successful, you win false
friends and true enemies,
SUCCEED ANYWAY
The good you do will be forgotten tomorrow,
DO GOOD ANYWAY....

There are several other lines to this poem. Even though this poem may be a bit extreme I have found comfort in it. In my own experience I have found some people that I have tried to help have treated me with unkindness. That counselling or even loving people can be unappreciated. I have also learned that others unkindness may not be a reflection of me. That I still want to treat people how I wish to be treated. The Golden Rule so to speak. I do not always manage to be kind, I continue to work on trying to be so.

Chapter 2 Self-Reflective Questions:

* Who in your life, whether an author or someone you know personally has positively influenced your life? (It can also be a Character in a book or show). For example, I am a bit of a TV fanatic and I learn from various characters in shows. One of my favorite shows has been "Grimm" and I am inspired by the many strong characters in that show.

* Sometimes it might be useful to have an image or item on display that you will see to remind you of the strength of a character or of a real person that is inspiring you. In hypnosis this is called a post hypnotic suggestion or an anchor. In using the previous self-reflective question, for example: I have a small gem skull on my dresser that when I see the skull it reminds me of being a strong woman, as it reminds me of one of my favorite characters in the show the Grimm. Similar you might have a photo of someone that reminds you of strength on display. What is an object that could inspire you?

* What are some of the lessons these people or characters have shared or gems that you have held on to?

CHAPTER 3

Our First Child Moving Out

Taking our teen/young adult to her first job away from home I decided to ask my ex if he would go with our daughter and I to facilitate this move. She wanted to take her own car and was not comfortable with the idea of driving this far alone. I felt since it was a 3-person job as I would still need a vehicle to drive home or I would need a ride back. Our daughter's first job was to be a lift operator at a ski resort in the mountains several hours away from where we lived. My ex responded yes to my request of helping our daughter with the move and being one of the drivers. I was a bit surprised yet grateful knowing I too did not wish to do this journey alone.

Our daughter had been fighting with her dad around the time - at that time he was her primary home. They had both taken to saying: "I can't wait for you to go".

"I can't wait to go".

I think this was partly due to my ex's belief that once 18 a child should leave the home. I do not hold this same belief and she was aware she could stay with me. She decided an adventure would be in order. It is also a developmental task that a person of her age would push away her parent(s) to instill her own independence.

For the first number of hours she stayed with me and travelled in my vehicle while he drove her car. We all seemed in good spirits.

Part of my story is I left my husband due to "my sensitivity" to his drinking. Once we crossed the border, our daughter would be of legal drinking age. My ex on the road came from her car and offered our daughter a beer. I don't know if he thought this was funny, but we were not amused. He had plans to go out drinking with friends that night. She said, "No thanks".

Then he stated, "Ask your mom if she wants a beer?" He knows I no longer drink.

As mentioned I am not sure if he was trying to be rude or funny?

My daughter stated, "You better not drink dad, you are driving my car!"

Then we proceeded on our journey.

The first night my daughter and I stayed with my cousin and my ex stayed with friends. The next morning, we met up for breakfast which was nice, and it felt like being a family again. He bought which was appreciated. Then we went to buy some groceries for our daughter and a shovel for her car since she'd be living in the mountains and there would be snow. At this point my daughter, I believe, became nervous – I think the reality of moving out and having to buy her first groceries 'hit her'. I gave her some money to help pay for the shovel and groceries.

Because at this point, she was in my opinion uptight with me, I suggested she jump into her car with her dad. He had beer stacked in the passenger seat. So instead they both got into my vehicle and I drove her car.

We made it to the ski lodge where she was to work. She found someone to show her her room. The room was nicer than she expected so that made for a good start.

Also, she discovered she hadn't brought too much stuff which was a fear of hers. (Aside: her birth sign is Cancer so a home is important.)

Then we went for a meal and bought a baby gift for a friend that was expecting. By this time, it was snowing hard. My ex suggested we get a picture with our girl, this was nice and it turned out to be a lovely photo. As we left our daughter at her new home I had tears well up and I was a bit surprised by my tears. Our baby was no longer a baby.

On leaving our daughter, my ex had me drive. It was snowing steady and I am a nervous driver in these conditions, but I drove. It was busy traffic in the nearby city and where I drove my ex to stay at his cousin's, the location was more rural with quite a few sloughs. I was anxious but managed to get him to where he was staying and find my way back to my cousin's in the snow storm. I was exhausted by the time I arrived.

The next morning, I was awoken by my cousin's two youngest children wanting to play and by their jumping on my bed with me in it! Later the one had Tim Horton's hockey, so they left, and I relaxed and made muffins. One of my talents is making muffins without a recipe and with ingredients I can improvise from. I left the muffins as a gift for having hosted me.

My ex called and asked if I was ready. I told him I could be and inquired where he wanted to meet within the hour. I love my GPS, yet they do at times give the wrong directions. Luckily, I saw the building where I was going so knew to ignore the GPS.

Once I picked up my ex we went to get coffee for the

road. While he was waiting he noticed steam coming from my engine. My radiator cap had been loose, likely from my pre-trip oil change and all of my engine coolant was gone. Fortunately, my ex knew what to do so we picked up some coolant. We ended up using a gallon and a half and we checked it a few times en route. I told my ex several times I was glad he had been there as I may not have caught the problem and what could have happened if I was on the road not near road service.

We took turns driving home, there was snow. About half way home I opened up the topic asking why he did not try with me? He said because he was just not into it. I shared we had bad timing. When I wanted to try he hadn't wanted to and when he wanted to try I felt it was too late. His counsellor had shared he was not ready when once in our separation we had considered trying again. Once after our separation we had also gone for family counselling and again we seemed on different pages. On the drive I had some physical stress, tummy issues, and I voiced we hadn't really given it a real chance.

He replied he thought we had, yet at other times he had voiced otherwise. I felt better for this bit of direct chat and said I would try and let him go. (The difficulty being able to let him go has been a reoccurring theme for me.) It's hard to stop loving someone and I today realize you can still love someone and let them go.

I also shared I knew he was working with a match maker. He asked how I knew, and I stated how do you think I know? It was our daughters of course. I asked how this was going. I suggested he give some feedback to his matchmaker that he shared with me as it likely would help her do a better job.

It had been 2 days since our trip. I had felt tired, but I was glad we did this as a family. My ex said a friend of his was jealous that we were able to get along as his friend could not get along with his ex. I mentioned one of my friends that had shared this same sentiment. (This last part was written a few years ago and through our divorce there have been times we have taken steps apart and been less involved with each other and other times still attend events together.)

I thought about when after our trip when I had dropped off my ex at his home (where we as a family had lived), that I had gone inside to speak with our youngest daughter. She had stayed there to care for the dog, she had been 'short' and mean with me. The next night she voiced how she doesn't like seeing us together at each other's houses. I am glad she was able to voice this as I did not realize this was difficult for her. She shared this several times throughout the years. This must have been confusing for her and I believe this has been confusing for us as well. I reassured her that we are not back together and that we are trying to be friends and that this is not her choice. Much like how children are not able to choose if a family remains together.

My oldest child gave me the impression that both of her parents driving her to her first away from home job had been a comfort to her.

Chapter 3 Self-Reflective Questions:

*   Have you and your ex ever tried marriage or family counselling?

*   If you did, did you find any benefits with the counselling? If so what benefits did you find?

*   Are you able to do things with your ex for helping out in the raising of your children or for extended family members?

*   When you do spend time together with your ex what sort of feelings or thoughts does this raise/ or bring out?

*   If difficult or reignited feelings arise what do you do to cope with these feelings?

*   Are you aware that your children/ or loved ones might be confused by seeing you as an ex-couple doing things together?

*   Does other's opinions of this matter?

*   What could you do to try to have a better relationship with your ex for the benefit of yourself and for your children?

CHAPTER 4

Leftovers and being Blind to the situation

I am more aware now how having had a dysfunctional family of origin played a role in my divorce.

As already mentioned, 'Leftovers', is a term from the book, "Rebuilding-when your relationship ends." The original author, Bruce Fisher. In referencing this book, the original edition had the forward written by Virginia M. Satir and if memory serves me correctly Virginia is an authority of the effects of alcoholism on the family and where the whole family is involved in therapy.

I have since about the age of 11 known that my family suffered from alcoholism and around age 14 began to learn about the family illness of addiction. It wasn't until about age 18 that I could finally admit to both of my parents having alcoholism. I took a while to break through the protective nature I had towards my mother and self-admitting to her own addiction. The book by Robert J. Ackerman, "Same House, Different Homes: Why Adult Children of Alcoholics Are Not All the Same", may shed some light on this.

Both of my parents were chronic alcoholics/addicts. As a result, information about children raised in a home such as mine, suggests that I would be more susceptible to finding a love relationship with someone that was prone to addiction. My partner (we were married 25 years) in my heart is likely prone to being an addict, but like my mother he never has held onto this diagnosis/term), but I can say his use "bothered me". My mother to her dying day though grossly deteriorated due to her drinking/pill use never admitted to having a problem. My ex at times has thought he might have addiction but is more prone to refute this.

Let me just say Addiction is not a moral issue it is or can be a medical diagnosis. That one trait of this illness is the person often afflicted by addiction may not even recognize the problem. It is highly treatable if the person is able to address that a problem exists. I am a huge believer in prevention such as educating those that have the genetics to be susceptible to this illness in the best-case scenario abstain from drinking to ward off the potential of progression of said illness. Unfortunately, due to the nature of this disease those likely to be afflicted appear to want to utilize mood- and mind-altering chemicals hoping they would not develop the disease.

When I met my husband, he knew but I do not think he understood how much I had been affected by this family disease even though on our very first meeting I tried to inform him of this. He even later attended a self-help meeting for family members of alcoholics in effort to get to know me. Also, we had a dry wedding (not quite as his friends snuck alcohol into the dance), my intent was to have a dry wedding as my mother had died the year prior due to her own addiction and I did not want alcohol at our wedding.

So, forward many years later, prior to my leaving my husband. Both of my daughter's unknown to each other had sat on the same couch a week apart crying about their father's drinking. Around this same time, it was the first time in our marriage, where I chose to sleep on the couch due to some meanness he said to me. I tried to not be noticed by our children this particular night. My youngest however got up to use the bathroom and noticed me on the couch and both approached me the following morning to ask if daddy and I were getting a divorce. I'm not sure if I already had this idea to divorce their dad; but, I do remember thinking "out of the mouth of babes".

Back to leftovers, I used to beg my mother to leave our dad. I still wonder if she had would she have sobered up and lived? She died at age 59. I have many thoughts regarding this and will leave these for now.

Having my children, being impacted by parental drinking, I believe was a huge reason for my leaving someone I loved. I did not want my children to experience the ill effects of alcoholism in the home. Granted through my naivety I did not realize they would still be influenced by the other parent as we would continue to parent together. At least in my own home I would be able to not have drinking under my roof. Fortunately, he did rise to the occasion of being a better dad, managing his anger better. He did not quit drinking. I think all of us – our girls, my ex and I would agree his becoming a nicer person to be around was the gift out of the "shit" of divorce. I just wish this shift had occurred while we were still married then we likely could have avoided all of this hurt.

I am a big believer in we are souls having a human experience here to learn lessons. This dissolving of our marriage has been a doozy.

After our split I can recall looking back and seeing so many of our mistakes. As the cliché states: "hindsight is 20/20". I have found even looking back it may take many glances to get the lesson(s) or clearer vision.

I remember a dear friend of mine when she left her husband as he had turned violent. He also had addictions. In my role as a counsellor I actually helped her, and her daughter find a 'safe house'. It was when her husband turned violent involving their daughter she had the strength to leave. Even in sorrow there can be humour. The safe house I took them to had been largely decorated by my own friend. She had given items to charity and here some of these items were decorating her new temporary home! We did discover this decorating coincidence the night she moved into the "safe" home! I watched over the months where she maintained her integrity while he broke rules. For instance, the judge ordered a hold on their joint bank account and he withdrew all of the funds. Through tears and her strength, I knew divorce was not to be taken lightly. I remember her words, "divorce is hell, are you sure you are ready for this?"

I don't think anything could have prepared me for this. And it seems to me we tried family counselling after separating. Too late for sure. I remember 'the talk' months before our actual split. (I had a typo that I corrected that said splat rather than split perhaps this is more accurate). I had chosen a restaurant that was not a favourite should I choose to not go there again, and I have not. During this talk I used the word divorce and tried to tell my husband how unhappy I was. He wanted me to agree to 3 things: 1) That I not egg shell walk anymore, 2) That we do more as a couple and 3) That we fight more. At least this is what memory I have of the conversation. For 1) and 3) I said I will not quit egg shell walking as I do this at times out of fear and I believe for safety and I couldn't see how fighting would help, stating I would rather stick to having conversation. As for point 2) He has not been easy to be with.

After what I deemed as our "Divorce talk" nothing seemed to change I felt in some ways it got worse as I did not see effort on his part. I believe I saw this lack of effort on his part as a sign of my needing to move on. I believe I told him that I wanted him to get help with anger management as his behaviours at times had been scary.

I did not see change and attributed this to his lack of effort. Several months later I had met a fellow that was Interested in me and this other person spoke of wanting to hold my hand. I had spoken to my husband previously before meeting this person how hurtful it was to me that he, my husband no longer wanted to hold my hand.

One day my then husband was tying his shoes and stated his friends thought there might be another man. I responded that there is but at the moment we are only friends. He left saying as he went how that hurt. I wish he would have taken more issue with this and that we had faced it head on. I believe because he did not pursue this further that I decided I was not that important to my then husband.

Another time I call it the 'Walk and stomp', we went for a walk and neither of us realized how angry I was until this walk. I had thought our marriage was over and he a few months later approached me I think wanting to work on us. I was incensed, and I was thinking this is a little too late! And thus, on the walk I stomped. We later ended up going to a Tim Hortons and I don't recall if we walked or drove. We wrote down a list of what actions we would do to reconnect. I wrote it on a napkin. No idea where that napkin is but it included things like dates, going for a bike ride, likely walks.

We did follow through on a bike ride and it was the best! I had real hope and rekindled my feelings for him, enjoying the sunset and laughing as his bike chain fell off as he drove into a flock of geese to scare them. Unfortunately, the only 2 dates I remember were in my view disasters. One we went to what had been a favourite restaurant, we went for dessert thinking it would be cheaper. Wish we had invested more on dates, I would rather have spent money on dates than on a divorce. On one of our dates during dessert he started to talk about our finances and my eyes began to water. I told him I thought we were on a date, and how I was discouraged that this was the topic of conversation. I stated we could have this type of conversation at home. I had hoped we would be bonding. The second date I remember was a sports function where he was so drunk and though he had me sit on his knee, I felt I couldn't continue to live like this. I think that same night he brought the party to our home and I was discouraged.

Our split ended up being in December before Christmas, the timing was not planned. We had decided to split after a weekend away together. We decided we needed to tell our children we were splitting. We sat down and did this together, it was heart breaking for all of us. After he said he wanted us to be the best divorcing couple ever. In many ways we did handle things with integrity, though in retrospect I further complicated things by getting involved with the fellow that let me know he was interested in me far too soon. This confused our children. I believe my daughters blamed our split on him even though they seemed to have forgotten there was already trouble. I have since learned that my daughters blamed the divorce on me. I also now see where an outsider would have been more respectful to leave me alone at this difficult time.

After our split we took the kids sledding at a nearby hill. As a family we had fun. The kids walked up ahead of us. We were talking, and my ex asked why I hadn't hit him over the head with a 2 by 4 (piece of wood). I responded that I thought I had metaphorically. I had let him know how I was feeling. He said no that he meant literally I should have hit him over the head with a board. It is sad that when one of us was hurting it was not obvious to the other.

For this reason, when I work with couples I try to advocate for both sides in an effort to help each side to hear the seriousness of each other. We did try some family counselling. I think we had already split. The counselling agency had noticed both our girls on the waiting list so noted it was a family. They reached out to us and asked if we would be interested in having some family counselling to assist new psychiatrists in training. We went maybe 2-3 times. One student at a time would work with us in one room. The others were behind a one-way mirror observing and if they wanted a colleague to ask something they would knock on the door. After we would switch rooms and we would observe their observations they had about us. It was somewhat fascinating. Our girls were so brave! I was impressed with one student. He had told us that he could not understand why we would be separating when to him it was so obvious that there was still love there. I felt bad for the student as I felt this was an accurate statement. Yet his clinical supervisor more or less scolded him for his insight. I would have liked to have helped this student in his education and would have backed him against his supervisor. At the time I was the subject, we were being observed and I believe I just did not have the energy at the time.

Again, more wishing we could have turned things around at that time.

After our separation I joined a divorce group. It was a lay led (not professionally led) group. It was supposed to be a non-denominational or non-specific religious group and I found this not to be the case. I will not share the title of the group. It was horrible. Because I made a commitment I finished the series. I found it abusive emotionally and partly set up to induce guilt. Had I been stronger I would have simply not attended.

There were 2 points I did take from the group. The first is that I was the only one out of the group that admitted to still loving my partner. At this time my ex had sent me a letter talking about not changing the past but that we can re-define our ending. I had mistakenly thought he wanted to try again. We clarified this over tea. The others in the group appeared to hate their ex's and this difference was pointed out to me many times in the group.

The second lesson from this group was that for every 5 years in the relationship it takes about 1 year of healing.

I thought I have all sorts of clinical therapy skills so thought I could do it quicker. I was wrong and found this to be a fairly accurate time frame. We were married 25 years, so this formula would suggest 5 years of healing. I was on year 6 of healing at the time of this paragraph and there had been lots of healing, but I was still struggling. I guess a third gift from this group was that I made a male friend. Having a friend of the opposite sex in a platonic relationship was encouraged in this group. I approached one member and he agreed to try friendship and is a friend until this day. He did admit eventually he had hoped for more than a platonic relationship at the time. I was flattered and am glad we were able to just stick with a friendship.

Our actual breakup occurred at a resort where my then husband won a free weekend. Driving up north to the resort we talked about alcoholism and he did not see my concern. At a rest stop we gassed up our vehicle and the bathroom lock on the door was broken. I told my spouse about the broken lock and that I myself had left the door ajar when I used the facility. He either did not hear me or didn't realize that shutting the broken knob would have consequences. In any event he was trapped inside the washroom and it wasn't until a person working there broke the doorknob with a screwdriver that he could be released. I thought it was quite funny. My then husband did not see the humour at all.

Once at the resort I felt that we had beautiful accommodation. My then husband did not find the accommodation to his liking. I found it discouraging to be around this negativity.

We had for the most part an amazing weekend. I shared some of my personal energetic self by "toning" or "singing" to a nearby herd of elk that seemed pleased by this. We loved each other that weekend and enjoyed swimming. At meals he would order alcohol, I felt hurt by this as he knew I did not like to be intimate if there was drinking. I noticed an older couple where the husband appeared to be trying to impress the waiter and it also appeared his lady friend or wife was unimpressed, thinking to myself, would that be my future?

That weekend on the radio there was a song by Fefe Dobson, called 'Stuttering' in the lyrics there was the message to tell the truth if you ever really cared about your partner. I felt a need to tell my then husband I felt there was someone else in my heart. I voiced this to him and once I did, rather than talk about it he insisted we leave. We packed up in the wee hours of the morning and drove home. On the drive it appeared that we both tried to convince each other we are not right for each other and would be better off separating. I believe a part of me was trying a, "last ditch effort", to reach out and resolve our relationship and work together. I'm not sure what was going on for him, other than hurt and all the way home he did try to state splitting is likely for the best and I may have been stunned rightly or wrongly. That was the end of us. Soon after our conversation of us splitting up took place with our girls.

I was also confused as justifying our split turned to my then husband wanting me out of the house as his anger seemed to settle in. I was advised by a lawyer I did not need to vacate. We agreed on each would leave for a night or two so that one parent remained, and the children did not need to move. A huge hurt and something I still do not have resolution over is my then spouse when he spent his night or two away moved in with what I would have considered my family. (I had been their nanny at the time my spouse and I met, and they considered us somewhat as family. I had been their babysitter for years before they met my future husband.) Why did he not move in with his parents? Even his mother before she died had wondered the same thing. To further complicate this these people seemed to wonder why I had not reached out to them? I had felt they had chosen to support him. I felt they had chosen sides, and this has remained a theme for me throughout our divorce.

I ended up getting an opportunity from a friend to house sit for her parents while her parents were away on a holiday while trying to sell their home. My oldest refused to stay nights with me and my youngest did spend some nights. It was a horrible ache to not have my children full time. I had been the primary parent and at times even being a single parent when my then husband would go away weeks to months at a time guiding fishermen and hunters. I am grateful for the most part that we have shared parenting since the divorce. Initially I felt like, "a duck out of water".

I want to mention after our divorce there was a play at a theatre where I had season tickets and the show was based on a couple going to a resort and the show primarily focused on the near dissolving of their marriage. It was sooo déjà vu, it was one of the hardest plays I have ever seen. In fact, my girlfriend did not realize the impact this play had on me. I had cried all the way throughout the play. Even during intermission, I cried sitting on a chair out in public as others mingled. My friend had not realized and a few days later called me rude saying she could not find me at intermission and I left immediately after the play. I told her I had been out in the lobby during intermission and I had cried through intermission and through the entire play and left right after to avoid being seen. I thought she had seen or been aware of my distress. I later realized I had been a silent crier and she had not noticed. In the play the couple saved their marriage, and this was a bitter reminder that we had not.

In the upcoming chapters I hope to share incidents that we have had to navigate as a divorced couple. I wish I had some guidance towards these types of occasions. I am a trauma expert and have helped many people to cope with their own pain and turmoil. It is my hope in sharing some of my (our) story that others may be comforted, given hope and perhaps better understanding of what they too may go through of a similar nature. There was and maybe still is a TV comedy show I believe is called "Reba", with an actress of the same name where she lives next door to her ex and his new wife. Perhaps I should have watched that show to better prepare myself. If you already know how to deal with the things I hope to share about – good for you. Feel free to send me your own stories and wisdom. I know writing this fulfills my need to be a helper and hopefully will serve me as being a cathartic experience for me. Some of my best learning as already mentioned is by hearing from other's experiences helping me to navigate my own.

Chapter 4 Self-Reflective Questions:

* Leftovers are things from your own childhood that may negatively impact your marriage. For me the largest left over was having parental addiction in my family of origin home making me more sensitive to a partner's drinking. What are some leftovers that you are aware of that may have influenced your marriage?

* Are you able to recognize the distress your partner is showing in your marriage?

* Do you feel they can see your distress?

* Do they exhibit distress that you could be aware of?

* Are your children showing signs of being bothered by your "family stress" and or relationship discord?

* What might you do to better communicate the need/ want for change?

* Have you put effort into Counselling as a couple or as a family or even individually?

* Is there someone that can help you communicate to your partner?

* Have you tried any rejoining activities with your partner? If so what have you tried?

* Do you still have feelings for your ex? If so what are the feelings?
    Do your feelings come and go?

* How many years were you together, include time together before marriage. Divide this number by five – the suggestion made to me was for every five years together you will likely require a year for healing. If together 25 years divide by five equals a suggested five year framework for healing. What do you think of this formula?

* Who has been the primary parent, involved in the day to day care of the children? Are you aware that once separating/divorcing there will likely be a change in custody? If joint custody is decided, you will not see your children on a daily basis.

* For the sake of the children it is recommended parents cooperate and not speak badly in front of the children about their other parent.

* Remember all members of the family can each be hurting in their own way.

* What do you have in place to support your children? Are there grandparents/friends that can be made aware that the children may need their support and care at this time.

* We as parents informed our children's main teachers of the difficult time we were having in the family so if the teachers noticed anything they could be aware and possibly let us as parents know as well. I was grateful that one teacher reached out and let me know my child had been crying in the classroom.

     Will you be talking to teacher/s about concern for your children during this difficult time?

* Is there a show, a book or another resource that has helped you to prepare for the "initial shock" of separation/divorce?

* As a child had your parents separated/divorced? Do you remember how you found out?

     As a child what might have made the process easier?

* Are you prepared to try some of the above?

Dating

I decided to take a University summer session class and worked full time and found I really had no time for dating. I had a book, (I apologize I lent the book out forgetting the title), I found this book at a second hand book store I had never visited before. I am one of those people that believe a book will jump out at me if I am meant to read it. I enjoyed this book immensely. The author (again sorry I forget the title and author) had a theory that one should date 3 people at one time, sleep with no one (no sex) and that those involved are informed there are others. She proposed that this might bring out the competitive nature of the men where they may try harder to romance you. She also spoke of the bonding hormone given off during sex suggesting you abstain from sex so that oxytocin and your pheromones won't bond you to the wrong person prematurely. I felt it was a complete social experiment. Being in Psychology, I have been the type to try out what I learn to see if it is applicable or sound theory. For example, I attended a colleague's lecture on assertiveness once where she promised you do not need to give a reason for refusing a request, and that stating "no" is sufficient. I put this into practice one day with brutal results. I would say that of course one can say "no". It is more palatable if some sort of courteous response is attached even if it is as simple as, "I have personal commitments that I must attend to."

The date three theory was partially helpful. My own experience was hurtful to others and also to myself. The author had stated to keep your best options open as you date three and if one proves not to be a good match for you then break it off with that person and replace them with another. I signed up for on-line dating and initially I chose not to show my photo which was an option. I felt this let me be more in control of my choices. I discovered many on the site that I met did not look like their photos. In one case I did not even think it was the gentleman's photo at all. I can be blunt and when I met this particular man I told him he looked nothing like his photo, that I am not interested in dating him, but would be willing to stay for tea if he liked. I am guessing he was surprised by my directness. I met most of the men from the on-line site at coffee places so that it was in public and we could have a short visit and part ways after.

I did this process twice, the dating of three, over a two - year period two months each time. I had taken another summer session class both years. I only allowed myself a span of two months each time I dated three. It was fun, horrible and exhausting. What I learned from the first bout of dating online is that people do not necessarily show you their true selves. The second time I would request a meet as soon as possible as it is easier to see a fraud in person than online. "Eyeball to eyeball", so to speak worked better for me and yet even in person I was deceived. I did better the second time around.

The first time I discovered some only wanted sex

and if I could figure this out prior to a meet I did not meet the person. One fellow I met very much in public and he quickly told me he wanted to have sex, I let him know just as fast that this was not part of my process. He kept backing away, as if to run away, basically stating if I change my mind to let him know. I likely loudly stated "not going to happen". He was of a good profession on his profile if he was honest and I admit I was surprised by this encounter. My daughter has good "guts" and she even told me not to go meet this one as she had overheard our phone conversation as she sat beside me in a vehicle. Interesting as she had not much to go on. Online dating is not for the faint of heart.

Another gentleman I quite liked early on told me about his chronic depression. I knew that this would be a deal breaker for me because of my career. Please don't get me wrong I do have compassion, but due to my work I know how hard this can be on a relationship and since I was just meeting people I knew I was unlikely to pursue this relationship and I told him. It turned out I did date him a few times to get a feel for the severity of his issue as I really liked him. He ended up breaking it off (remember we were dating not committed). He said his reason for not wanting to see me again was that it was too hard on him knowing that I was seeing others. I thought fair enough and realized this is hard on someone that has decided they like you. I have not given it much thought, but I do know some of the men I dated were seeing others and we may have not discussed this, but they did appear to not like that I was so open about seeing others.

I also had one semi-dangerous situation. I met a

fellow on line that I did not want to date he still wanted to meet me. He is an amazing artist and so I agreed and told him it was because of his art. We had plenty of common ground, this plus he lived somewhere fascinating that I wanted to hear more about. He appeared smitten with me and I told him he was too intense for me and that I was not interested, reminding him I had told him this all along. He told me he wanted to be my "champion". He wanted to walk me to my car I said no thank you but did walk him to his car. I did not want him knowing which car was mine. He tried to kiss me, and I ducked and said good bye. I could see he was still watching me. Rather than going to my car I went into a business (food type) that was closing and asked if I could be there, while they cleaned to close, telling them why I needed their assistance. He did not drive away for at least half an hour. I have no idea if he hid to follow me. I am grateful that once home I texted him stating it was nice to meet him, that I found him too intense with me and I would not be in touch again. He responded in a nice way and fortunately he did leave me alone.

I do know on line dating from what those I have met or have shared some disastrous results of their on-line dating experiences such as: rape, also being set up thinking they (men) are meeting a woman and getting beaten by a man. So please be as safe as you can. I realize I could have been hurt and am grateful I managed to be safe as I have not always made the soundest of decisions in life let alone with dating.

I met a fellow in the traditional way, I was out for a walk and he was biking, and he followed me as he had been with friends and caught up to me on his bike. He asked for my number. I did not have paper, he started to write it with a rock on the road and I asked him not to as I didn't want my number written on the road. He did manage to exercise his memory and called me. He requested a meet. I agreed, and we had plenty in common. He stated he was a medical doctor that moved here from another county and needed to re write his exams. Part of me was impressed with this. We dated only a few short weeks, but I felt something was off. I met him in public to break it off. He was surprised. I told him I could not really put my finger on why, but that I had decided to no longer see him. That is when he told me he was actively married living with his wife and children. He originally told me they were back in his home country and divorced. He thought being honest at that time I would appreciate his honesty and give him another try. I told him no it only confirms my "guts". I never saw him after that even though he continued to try and text me. I ran into him once on a walk and refused to talk to him even though he followed me a bit. I decided that meeting someone the 'old fashioned way' was not that great either.

After my first bout of the online dating I had narrowed it down to my favourite three and then chose one. I remember the day I told my second choice that I had chosen another. He was somewhat hurt by this, but I think he had another lady he was also interested in. My main reason for not choosing him was I had taken him to an event and another woman (she was married) kept hitting on him and he seemed to enjoy this immensely even though he was my date. We have spoken of this on occasion. We have a pet name for this lady that makes us laugh. When he and I originally met his marriage had recently ended and he had been at that point I believe craving the attention of other women as his self-esteem took a huge dive in his marriage ending. I am pleased to say we are still good friends and have wonderful discussions about relationships and life. I am grateful to have met him on-line.

Unfortunately, the fellow I chose from the first group ended up being a fraud. What he presented me with was mostly lies. This plus he wanted me to move to his town and wanted me to have a child with him. I had no intention of having more children and in many ways this fellow was a child and did not have time for the two or three he already had. We did have a few good dates; however, it became apparent he was not for me. We had spent quite a bit of time conversing by computer and by phone I was so mad at myself that it took me a few weeks once we met to see the truth. My friends say good thing it only took two or three weeks to "see the light" so to speak. This is where I made the rule the next time I tried on-line dating to plan to meet those I met quite quickly face-to-face.

I was a bit immature at that breakup. I sent him a YouTube song as a rebuttal. He thought the title was a compliment until he heard it and replied, "ouch".

The song was: Beyoncé, "The best I never had." I still love that song and video. I just happened upon it the night we broke up (Thanks Angels). In the song it talks about "dodging a bullet" as in glad that relationship never really happened.

The second time I tried online dating, a year after my first attempt, I did meet a wonderful man. Ironically, it was the night I cancelled my online membership. We met at a coffee shop in a bookstore. We had a lovely coffee, we might have even shared a dessert, I can't remember. I do remember thinking he did not look like his picture and I told him so and added that is not a bad thing. I found him handsome. We hung out looking at books after and there was a comfort about that. I was seeing others and he knew that. He did not pressure me.

We both went on holidays, he went to the Philippines to go Scuba Diving and I went to Mexico and my daughters joined me for a few days. Our time apart was good. He was in touch while he was away. I had a "milk run" return trip with all kind of stop overs and delays because of the snow. I arrived in my home city at 2am. Another person I was dating was to pick me up and due to the late hour, I told him not to bother. The fellow that had gone on a scuba trip was still on Philippine - time so he insisted on picking me up. That was when I stopped seeing others (I think that was February). I never agreed to be exclusive until one day in April when I decided I really did not wish to date others and I knew it would give us a better chance.

We use April 5, 2015 or Easter as our anniversary. Easter-New Beginnings. This date is also one day before my deceased mother's birthday, oddly enough. I think she would have liked him.

Now just because we agreed to be exclusive did not mean I never questioned our being together. I am more settled into our being a couple; however, it still is not a given. I found I did question if this relationship was meant to be on a regular basis for the first few years and do much less so now. I do not question our relationship as much as I initially did. I have taken forever to get on with allowing myself to accept I am a divorced woman and that my ex husband will no longer be my partner. I attach easier than some and watching my grown daughters they also share this trait. I am pretty sure my reservation is that I really don't want to go through all the hurt of separating from a strong relationship bond.

My new man is what I choose to call him. My fear is not about him it is about my own insecurities and "left overs". Even though I was hesitant at the beginning, I still chose to stay in this relationship. I knew from the get go that he is a good man. Previously I have tended to go for the "bad boys" and that this is a part of my history. I knew my new man would be and is good for me so rather than "flight" or run away I live in this relationship one day at a time (ODAT). Currently we do not live together, and we are five years into our relationship. We do talk about possibly moving in together, at this time I am not ready, and I am not certain he is.

I have never had a man treat me so good. He is consistent and affectionate. He is intelligent and interested and interesting. My children both appear to love him, and they shared with me that they thought a few years ago when he and I headed for a holiday that they thought we were going to elope. My daughters told me they would never forgive me if I were ever to get married without them. I told them I am not ready to get married and that it is good and duly noted that if I ever do they will both be there.

One of my best friends was invited by her then fiancé to elope and she had the belief that marriage is about community and that with so many family members that she needed to include family. I can't speak for others I can see her and my daughters' points of view. My own father when he remarried after the death of my mother eloped and, in a way, I think this bothered me. Yet I was an adult at the time.

Chapter 5 Self Reflective Questions:

*   Are you interested in a new relationship?

*   Did you know it is recommended you be happy with yourself and not in "need" of another before you decide to date again?

*   Have you a "picture" of what you want in a love relationship? I am not referring to looks at this point but rather I am referring to personality traits. Have you made a list? Do you also share these traits? For example, if you want honesty in a partner are you yourself an honest person?

*   What are your ideas about dating?

*   Do you have some opinions on where you stand with levels of intimacy on dating?

*   If you are open to being sexual, do you plan to practice "safe-sex"?

*   Will you introduce your children to whom you are dating? See Chapters 9, 19 and 23.

*   What do you know about on-line dating?

* Are you aware that there are some con artists that are on-line pretending to seek love when really it is your money they are after or to cause harm?

* What safety protocols will you put in place when you are dating?

* The term, "Cat Fishing", I believe refers to someone pretending to be someone else on line.

* Do you care to share about your experiences with conventional and on-line dating?

CHAPTER 6
Death

I had no idea how having a loved one die after divorce would be or could be so difficult. In 2015 I had a good friend die and my mother in law and a sister in law die within a month of each other. I was close to the first two. I was actively involved in the first two visiting them up until the end. In fact, I was the last to be with my mother in law before her passing. I was too shy to sing but did hum some beautiful songs to her prior to her passing encouraging her to go home to God. I am not a religious person, but she is, and I am a spiritual person, so this was of great comfort to me. My mother in law was a mom to me. I knew my mother in law longer than I knew my own mother in terms of time on this earth. My Mom died when I was 20. I knew my mother in law for 29 years. My mother died of the horrible disease of Alcoholism so in many ways I lost her years before her death.

My mother in law died from pancreatic cancer and it went relatively quick where in the end she was skin and bone and no longer her vibrant self. Her actual death was a blessing. I was likely the closest of the daughters in laws to my mom (mother in law). This was likely due to the other daughters in laws having their own mothers, at least those that lived nearby. Mom would invite me to Mother's Day Tea's, and we would spend quite a bit of time even after the divorce together. She told me she did not want to lose me after the divorce and I felt blessed.

One of my friends cried when in my mother in law's passing I was not mentioned in the obituary. I did not feel as hurt as my friend did on my behalf. Apparently, my mother in law wrote her own obituary and I'd prefer to think she did not know the protocol (if there is one) on how to include a divorced in law in those who have survived the deceased. I love(ed) her very much and I do believe she knew this.

Before I continue with my mother's (mother in law) death I feel a need to go back to where my father in law predeceased her. He was the first to die after our divorce. My father in law and I were not as close, yet we did have a loving relationship. His and my relationship was not as easy. This was a large part of us having such different beliefs. He was a very Evangelical Christian, right from the start of my dating his son, my father in law to be, disapproved of my Catholic upbringing. I did not understand that the religion I was raised in he would judge as polar opposite. We agreed to disagree many times. At times he would share his beliefs with our children and I felt a need to give my daughters a different perspective. Since this book is not about "faith" I will spare the details. Let it suffice that we were not as close. As I got to know him more over the years I did have a better understanding of him. In some areas he even softened which was greatly appreciated. In fact, once he met one of the men I dated after our divorce and he was very gracious. He and I did share some common interests such as our children, flowers, puzzles, yard work and making relish.

At my father in law's (dad's) funeral it was a hugely difficult day for me. I was asked to do the funeral flowers. I had been trained in Japan in Ikebana - the Japanese art form that includes flower arranging. When my ex-husbands parents visited us in Japan when we were married, his parents attended a flower arranging class with my sensei (teacher). It was a high light for them and myself. My sensei treated them to lots of carnations to practice arranging and a lovely meal afterwards.

At the funeral I did not know if I would be allowed to sit with the family. As it turned out I did not sit with my daughters or with my ex. My ex had a new girlfriend who sat with them. It was weird to see him comforted by someone other than me as that had been my role for years. I sat with his cousins and other family members. I was particularly grateful for one cousin that invited me to sit with him. As we walked down the row of chairs it was weird as I randomly ended up being behind my children a few rows. I was able to admire the flowers and my father in law's siblings singing as we had this as part of our lives for our 25 years of marriage.

After the funeral I honestly don't remember details like the reception. I do remember seeing some of my ex's friends that had been our friends (mostly from his sports team) and that was wonderful. Some made the point of letting me know how much they missed me. Then a sister in law who travelled from Ontario when I saw her I said, "I'm sorry, but I have to leave", before she could say anything. I am not sure if I was afraid she would say something hurtful, but I was at the point of overload and left as I felt like crying, it all felt overwhelming.

When we had buried my father in law I was on one side of the grave with our daughters and my ex and his girlfriend were on the other side. When my daughters were crying my ex brought his girlfriend with him while he comforted the girls. Her being in such close proximity was difficult for me.

When his mother died we were at the same grave yard and I had shared prior that his bringing his girlfriend to us was very difficult and invited him to be aware of this. At his mom's funeral he did come to comfort our girls but left his girlfriend (a different lady than he'd been dating when his father passed) on the other side of the grave. This was appreciated. In fact, the first time for me to meet his new girlfriend was at his mother's prayers the night before. I felt like I lost my own mom, not an in law as previously mentioned. I was grieving her death and did not feel a need or desire to meet his new girlfriend (another type of loss for me). Though I acknowledged her I did not shake hands or visit her. My ex did not understand this.

In fact, a few months later, his family were planning a come and go tea for those that had not made it to the funeral. I had every intention of going to this tea to support my daughter, our other daughter was not able to be there. Prior my ex called and asked a favour that I hang out with his new girlfriend at this tea. I told him I would not. That I was still having a hard time seeing him with someone else. That it's good that the girls are accepting her and that he does but that it is not a requirement of me to get to know her. For this reason, I did not attend this come and go tea. On a couple other occasions following, I let it be known I was ready to meet her if he wished. One time we arranged to meet during a concert intermission that our daughter was performing in. The day prior I received I believe it was a text cancelling. I later found out it was because they broke up. We, my boyfriend and I did see my ex and visit during this intermission. My ex and my boyfriend did meet at another event when our daughter won numerous awards. They had several short meets when we ran into each other. My ex was always gracious. He even congratulated my boyfriend on winning over our youngest daughter on one occasion.

Recently at another funeral again on my ex's side of the family (his uncle's funeral) I told my ex I would visit with his girlfriend if he liked, that I felt ready and she was there with him. He told me not to bother and again I later found out they were broken up and she came because she liked his uncle. I had seen a cousin of my ex's there and did not get a chance to visit her as she had already left when I looked again. She and her husband had also divorced since our last seeing each other and I had not seen her in quite some time.

I found it a bit hard at this funeral as my ex gave a good speech and I enjoyed his humour missing the man I once had a life with. I had not known where I would sit at the reception and my daughter encouraged me stating she would sit with me. I felt grateful and we ended up sitting with my ex's brothers and sister in laws. There was no room left at the table and I offered to squish together to make room for my ex and his girlfriend and he stated no worries as he sat at another nearby table. There are dynamics with my ex in laws and I cannot speak for them as I do not know how they feel. One of my sister in law's that passed did hold a grudge telling my ex that I had hurt him, and he defended that stating that it took two and I only know this because he shared this with me. He also told her if she wanted to see our children she should include me as the girls would be more likely to visit her then. This never occurred. I do not hold a grudge as I know divorce is confusing for many.

They (I'm not sure who they are) say that divorce is more difficult than death. Try and tell this to a mother who lost her whole family in a car accident. I get the point though as with death there is a certain type of ending. With divorce the person can keep crossing your path. I myself would think I was healing (and I likely was). Grief or loss is a process not an event. I would sometimes be doing well moving forward in my life then I might see my ex or run into a mutual friend or hear about him from our children. Sometimes this was taken in stride but other times it would reopen old wounds, kind of like picking off old scabs and watching it bleed again. My mother used to say "don't pick" or it will leave scars. Likely advice I should heed. I have done better at letting the past go. Sometimes I revisit the past with new positive insights, other times it appears just to revisit the hurt. So, I caution you too reader. Carolyn Myss speaks of "woundology", essentially how some use their woundedness to hide behind and not necessarily move forward in her book, "Why People Don't Heal and How They Can." I have found I do better when I do not think too much about my past including my divorce. My divorce has been a part of my journey, but it does not need to define me. Even something as simple as filling out a form that gives the option of divorce or single. I check mark single as this fits better for me. As a counsellor some labels are useful as they may give me a whole bunch of information by using one or two words. The label however speaks of only part of a person. Say for example someone is diabetic, or alcoholic. The terms give me a gamut of information but that is only one facet of a person. I always remind my client's they are much more than the term, for example they are often, mothers/fathers, daughters/sons, teachers/educators, etc.

Joy Blossom, BA(Adv)Psy, C.Hyp

Chapter 6 Self-Reflective Questions:

* Have you had someone in your family or in your ex's family that has died since your separation/Divorce?

* Were you or your ex welcomed at the funeral/event?

* Did those in attendance treat you or your ex with courtesy and kindness?

* What might have helped you and/or them cope better?

* Could you have opted not to attend?

* Do you care to share about your own grief process?

* Were there children involved? How might have the children been better supported?

* Any thoughts on including the ex's in the deceased loved one's obituary?

CHAPTER 7

Some of the reasons for ending our marriage

Prior to our marriage this same sister in law I mentioned at the funeral, wrote me terrible letters about us "living in sin" as we lived together a year before marriage. My father in law wrote the same type of letters. Not exactly the way to build a healthy relationship with these people. It was also as if as soon as we married I was accepted, and I hadn't even changed, I was the same person. The last time I saw this sister in law was as already mentioned at my father in law's funeral. I had told her I was too upset to visit with her. She ended up dying I believe the same month as my mother in law a few years after my father in law. Prior to her death I wrote and sent her a nice card wishing her well in the circumstances of her dying. I never heard back. I was glad I had done this. It appears a huge part of my life lessons is for me to be kind even if others are cruel or unkind. I do not need to be intentionally mean. I have cut some people out of my life not to be mean but rather because I only have so much energy and would much rather spend my energy on those that have positive energy.

A huge quote that encouraged me to eventually be ok with our marriage separation (I still grieve this loss) is from the TAO Oracle by "Ma Deva Padma", St Martin's Press, New York, page 144:

"Simplify your life by eliminating anything that does not promote wholesomeness. You may be surprised to find that as you clean up your act you also start feeling better. Gradually eliminating whatever is no longer relevant- stuff, habits, relationships, or points of view – amounts to trimming the fat off your lifestyle. Consider what it would be like to live with the people and things that help you to feel good about yourself. Then consider the extent to which you are willing to go to make that a reality."

In my own words: I could not have imagined living with someone who was/is easy to live with??? Honestly, I could not imagine this. I had lived with many very difficult people. Granted there were some that were easier to live with; however, I lived with more that were difficult. I so wanted to live with kindness and courtesy if this was possible. At my original time of writing this I hoped it was possible. I have since found that this is possible. I do wish it had been with my then husband; but, for whatever reason this was not to be. He was extremely grumpy and unhappy, and I gave him a multitude of excuses or reasons for when he behaved poorly. Eventually I went with there must be a better way and my focus became about me.

I blame it partly on peri-menopause. Menopause has been seen as a second adolescence where again one can be self-focused and wanting what appears to be best for themselves. This is only an opinion and not necessarily science based. But when reading the first chapter of Christiane Northrup, M.D. Book – The Wisdom of Menopause, Creating Physical and Emotional Health and Healing During the Change. I related to how she no longer was all focused on helping her husband with his medical career and rather there was a shift on focusing more on helping herself with her own medical career. Christiane gave insights to where she had her own life change, some might call it a midlife crisis. I had wondered after reading about the hormone changes that once a woman changes she is not producing as much of the bonding hormones and as a result is considering her own viewpoint for a change. This was hugely eye opening for me. I wondered if I had read this book before leaving my spouse if I would have used this information in a manner that might have helped me stay in my marriage.

Christiane mentions a kind of peace in living in a "calmer" home after leaving her husband. I found much of my unsettled home energy has left since my leaving. I now own my own beautiful home and have much more settled energy in my home. Though my daughters have their own upsets in life it is different than the grumpy energy I had come to know in my marriage. I chose also to have a non-chemical use home where I chose to not let alcohol or substances into my home. This has bothered one of my friends. Most accept this or are not even aware of this as the topic never comes up. My oldest daughter was surprised that I was ok with her having a drink at a restaurant. I told her I have no control over what she does in terms of her own choices about drinking; but, rather I do not wish drinking in my own home.

Several months before separating my husband and I met at a not favourite restaurant of mine for what I called the "Divorce talk". I had prepared for this choosing a non-favourite location as I knew I would associate this difficult talk with the location. Months after this talk my then husband spoke of not realizing the significance of this talk. I could not imagine this. I recall most of what was said and the D-word (divorce) was used. My hope was to point out how unhappy I was and that I was considering leaving the marriage. He asked three things of me and I believe I could not agree to these three conditions. He wanted to have me "egg shell walk", less. Egg shell walking is when one tip toes around another's feelings in effort to try to not "set them off" or anger them. To this I replied I'd rather egg shell walk than to deal with his anger. I had been in the habit of usually after a negative episode, usually involving his unkindness to our daughters, I would approach him the next day and ask if he was aware how he was hurtful and point out what had happened. Then he would usually apologize within a day. Over time it would take 2-3 days for his acknowledgement. I did not ignore the bad behaviour I just chose to acknowledge it after a cooling down period. At one time he surprised me by stating he was aware how badly he had treated me yet made no acknowledgement of apologizing or of change. I believe this was a tipping point for me where I could no longer excuse his behavior out of tiredness or pain and I began to hold him more accountable.

Another condition he wanted was for us to spend more time together and to this my response was that he wasn't very nice, and this made it difficult to spend time with him. He did not holiday well and did not appear to know how to relax and appeared to resent me for not wanting a schedule on a break. I have enjoyed my holidays with girlfriends that can relax and have fun and we, my ex and I, had begun to holiday apart. He would go fishing, hunting with friends and I would enjoy time off with girlfriends. I believe having separated holidays did add to our relationship losing its bond.

Thirdly he wanted me to express my anger toward him more. To which I replied this does not seem safe to me. I also was in the habit of making all sorts of excuses for his negative behaviour. I would chalk it up to his being tired or in pain as he did suffer from a bad back. Yet I was aware that I tried to be accountable for my own behaviour. Because of my own childhood of dysfunction, both of my parents were alcoholics I think I put up with more negative behaviours because I loved him and saw his behaviours as part of the "disease" I believed he had. My compassion also likely hurt our relationship, as I may have not held him as accountable.

I had two friends that insisted my husband was alcoholic. They would say his negative behaviour was due to his being in between drinking episodes. I was not sure if this was true these two people stated they were sure this was the case. I did know his drinking bothered me. I had been a long-time member of a 12 step program because of my parents. I think I did not harp on drinking per se as I had learned there was nothing I could do about another's drinking. I instead focused on the unacceptable behaviour and how it related to me and our girls.

Several months after our not favourite restaurant talk I believe I had checked out of our marriage. For years I had done many things on my own. My husband had been a teacher and in summer he would often go up North to be a fishing guide while I stayed home caring for our children. People often commented as to why I would do this. Initially it was because I believe in a person finding their "bliss". I felt my husband was fortunate to do a job he loved, that his northern work was his bliss. I loved being a mom so didn't find this so bad. I also would get time off my own work when he was away, to care for my children, as the cost of paying for a sitter was prohibitive for this much of time. So often when he was away I would full time parent. I'm sure I worked some as I had a private practice by this point. I always found the first two weeks he was away and the first two weeks when he was home the hardest to adapt to. In general, I believe we adapted. This being apart did make it that we were both independent from each other and this likely added to our separation in the long run. As I knew I was able to function without him. The first two weeks he would be away I would miss him. The first two weeks he would return it would be an adjustment having him home as the girls and I would have established our own routine and had been thriving.

My husband grew unhappy with his teaching career. Initially I believe it had been a very satisfying career for him. He loved to teach grade 4. I was so impressed with his level of patience and creativity with this group. I was even invited into the classroom to help teach his unit on Japan as we lived in Japan together one year (one of our best as a married couple I would say). I would go into the class dressed in a Kimono and teach tea ceremony and other things.

As the years went by teaching changed. In addition to

teaching his students he was responsible for 2 profoundly disabled children (hearing and autistic) which brought in two Teacher Assistants (TA's). So essentially his job tripled. Not only was he teaching his usual group of children, but he also had to plan extra help for these 2 children and to instruct the two adult helpers. It was never his intention to be a special-education teacher. His love was teaching and this new dynamic I believe caused a lot of strain.

Eventually he took a year off to explore other careers. This was a stressful time for me as I thrive on knowing my basic needs are looked after and there was no guarantee of a wage. He did manage with several jobs to maintain an income it was just so uncertain. After a year away from his teaching career he did try teaching again. I believe he had given his grade 4 class to another teacher that wanted that grade and he was switched to grade 7 or 8. This grade would have extra challenges as developmentally at this age teens challenge adults as they prepare to become adults. My husband was not as suited in my opinion to be with this age of student. His father was a teacher and eventually a principal and I believe in the years that his father taught a teacher in those times could be physically threatening to get a student back in line. This is no longer the case and I think likely my husband struggled with the behaviours this age may have brought. Yet he was an excellent high school sport coach. These are just my theories.

After another year teaching he resigned and tried out other careers. I do not believe he had been settled career wise. I had never wanted to live in the small town we raised our family in as I have always been a city girl.

I was happier once we bought our own home in this town. Likely nicer than we could have afforded in the city. Having suffered some infertility, we had our first child ten years into our marriage the same month as our tenth year Wedding Anniversary. We were thrilled. We had lots of adjustments to make after having a child as previously we had pretty much lived for ourselves. Even though we were thrilled to have children we had been naive how this would affect us as a couple. One of our children was very hurt by a neighbour and rather than tackle this as a couple I attempted to deal with this myself. I should have allowed us to deal with this together. But because of my fear of my husband's anger I dealt with this alone. I believe this further split us apart as a cohesive couple. I had done the same thing with our infertility, I attended appointments in the city alone when I really should have asked him to attend with me. I would have liked the support yet told myself it is probably important he not miss work. And finally, our youngest almost died under the age of two and again I tried to cope with this mostly alone. The doctors did not know what the problem was. The doctors and care providers made many human errors and I tried to navigate this mostly alone. At one time we, our daughter and I, were hospitalized in the city as we were still breast feeding and I really could have used more support. I believe my own independence could have been a barrier in our handling issues together.

We, my baby and I, were also hospitalized a second time in our town. I recall one morning after being in palliative care for the night with her with no help from a nurse. This nurse and I had previously worked together at a green house and she had been a horrible person towards me. She ended up being our nurse and she did not help me once giving the excuse she had other patients to attend to. This was so unprofessional of her! The next day I called my husband and told him he must cancel his teaching that day and come to take care of our baby as I was exhausted as she and I had been up all night. I wish I knew how to accept help better but in this case the helper, the nurse, did not help.

So eventually, largely because of my husband's career ending we moved to the city as there was not enough work for my husband in the town. I had a job lined up for myself. Once we moved to the city this job was taken from me from a manager that did not realize I had been hired by another manager. This manager not the one that hired me, to the best of my knowledge held a grudge as many years earlier I had beat her best friend out in a job competition where her friend ended up having to leave the city seeking other work. I believe once this manager found out I was hired she did not allow me to claim this position, I had already seen my office and work. This was my best guess and later confirmed when a group of us had dinner out. A mutual friend did not believe this until he witnessed this himself at this dinner.

This meant we moved back to the city without either of us being employed. I took a job outside of my field and it was ridiculous. I worked for 100% commission and thus the company had me work an insane number of hours. I did well financially but not so spiritually, mentally or physically further adding to the stress of our marriage. I finally quit when I discovered another staff had been stealing thousands of dollars from me by changing the computer to claim my sales as her own. I have no idea how much she stole as it had not occurred to me that anyone would do such a thing. I was so glad to quit this job and get back to my family. The next job did not pay well and again it was an unhealthy atmosphere. The job was creative but lacking kindness and pay so I decided to go back into private practice and I have been doing this ever since.

The instability of a regular income added to the stress which I believe added to our relationship strain.

I have even wondered had my then husband remained happy in his teaching career if we would have been able to stay together.

Our separation is due to a combination of factors. As I mentioned earlier having a gravely ill child led me to be a very stressed out mama. At the time of having a sick baby and due to the stress, I went for what I thought was a massage. It ended up being a Reiki Treatment. I was only vaguely familiar with what Reiki was. I felt as if three years of stress left my body while having the treatment. The treatment ended up being a huge benefit to me and I instantly wanted to learn this treatment modality. This sent me on a new "Spiritual" path and this too likely aided in the dissolving of our marriage. My then husband was essentially, "freaked" by this new modality. After our marriage ended he was able to see Reiki as less of a threat, but his initial distain for it did add to the divide. After our separation/divorce, one day after his usual back treatment he was unable to walk and in great pain and he asked for a Reiki Treatment. I decided to charge him to emphasize the value. I would have gladly have given the treatment for free. He had been quite rude previously about my Reiki and I wanted to emphasize the value. He did pay me, and he did share it had helped. It is unfortunate he could not see it's benefit when we were together. I believe because of his non-acceptance of Reiki I chose to hide things of this nature from him as I no longer wished to be made fun of. This definitely further added to the divide.

Chapter 7 Self-Reflective Questions:

* What kinds of stresses in your lives may have contributed to the strain on your marriage?

* Is there anything you might have done, or can do, to alleviate the strain?

* Is there still similar strain in your life that you could attend to?

* What kinds of methods could help/do help you to cope better?

* Finances, lack of communication, beliefs, different ways of handling stress, infidelity (emotional and/or physical) are just some stressors in a relationship. Can you think of any more?

* Are you doing your part in self-care?

CHAPTER 8

The Other Man

I do not wish to further confuse the dissolving of our marriage. I need to share how a third party entered an already broken relationship. As previously mentioned I was forced to work at a job I did not like due to losing a job I had been hired for (end of last chapter). One of my colleagues at this new job was a bit of a "shit disturber". She encouraged me to cheat on my husband with a manager that made it obvious he wanted to be with me. I felt awful for trying to get my husband jealous at one of the parties the company had. I believe this was partly from this colleague encouraging me and my want or need of my husband's attention. Fortunately, I never cheated on my husband even though I had opportunity to on a business trip out of town.

After my daughter had already been sick and the mentioned hospitalizations I became interested in alternative healing methods. This was partly due to an elderly gentleman I met at the emergency waiting room with my daughter. He asked me what was wrong with my daughter? I told him they didn't seem to know, and I told him it might be her bladder. He did reflexology and showed me on her feet where to place pressure and directed me to do so nightly for several seconds per foot. Miraculously this appeared to be the resolution to her health problem and she was healed within two weeks.

Also, at that time I went for what I thought was a massage after the recommendation of a friend. I had been totally stressed and booked an appointment. I later found out rather it was a Reiki session I had booked. I felt like a whole 3 years of stress literally flew out through my feet and I felt calm and tranquil. I knew instantly after this experience that this was a technique or therapy I wanted to learn to do. I sought out a teacher.

My friend a doctor had told me about Reiki, she had broken her ankle and believed her ankle healed much faster due to Reiki. I took some training and was so impressed that I took all of my levels to become a Reiki Master. I practiced on friends and relatives. I never intended to use this on clients. One day I had a counselling client attend her counselling appointment. She had arrived with such back pain she could not sit down. I told her there is this thing I do and offered to try to help with her pain. She agreed, and I quickly gave her a 10 minute or so treatment as I wanted to get to the counselling which was her real reason for being there. The next day she called me and said, "I don't know what the 'F&%$' you did but whatever it was I have never felt better". It was at this time I contemplated adding this to my counselling practice.

Unfortunately, once I added Reiki to my practice I lost some clients as people appeared to fear what I did. I even volunteered to go to the clinic to inform doctors of what I was doing without any interest from the clinic. I lost some clients even though I did not push this modality on clients and to this day I still do not push Reiki. At the same time, I also played on a women's ice hockey team and the team's name was the "Stick Witches". I think this may further have added to people being afraid of the Reiki. I even had the team name on my license plate. A nun in the town did a similar treatment but people did not seem to see it as the same. I have and still do face people's fear in regard to this modality. I have also added Clinical Counselling Hypnotherapist to my credentials with a similar amount of fear and skepticism from some clients, friends.

Learning this new healing modality, Reiki, I believe also put a strain on my relationship with my husband. He was brought up Evangelical Christian (Mennonite Brethren), which I had limited understanding of and still do. He feared my Reiki and the new things I was doing. In retrospect I should have invited him into some events that may or may not have helped ease his fears. Initially I did invite him and at the time he was not interested. Around this same time a friend of mine that I later became the "best man" at his wedding, married a woman that was very pagan and a different type of healer. My husband did not like this couple. I later realized they were in essence partly responsible for encouraging me away from my marriage and encouraged me toward another man of similar metaphysical interests. The term twin flame was explained to me from them. I now have a better understanding of this term and felt once again I was misled. I must admit there was a huge pull towards this man. Also due to our weaker connection of my husband and I, I was vulnerable for this man's attention. I wish he would not have tried to be involved with me, a married woman. Yet I sometimes wonder if without this other man if I would ever have had the courage to leave my husband. The restaurant divorce talk took place months before meeting this other man.

Long story short, I did get approached by my husband in our kitchen as he was tying his shoes about to leave. He stated that his friends think there is another man in my life. To which I responded there is, and that this man is currently at this point a friend. My husband said that it hurts to hear that. Yet I do not think we addressed this situation. I had not yet gotten involved with this man at this point yet the lack of interest from my husband likely was a factor in me seeing this other man. Whether it makes sense or not I never slept with this man until after my husband and I separated. Yet being involved even emotionally with this man prior to our split totally complicated the issue. My children did not seem to remember us, their dad and I, having problems as a couple. They appeared to only see this other man as being the reason for our marriage breaking up.

I thought my children would remember what problems they saw in our marriage. Both of my children on the first time I slept on the couch in our marriage approached me in the morning asking if their dad and I were getting a divorce? I heard the girls and thought "out of the mouths of babes" partly wondering if they were wise beyond their years. This was early around when I began to first recognize we were in trouble in our marriage. This event took place months prior to my meeting the man I spoke of.

I will likely never forget the split of our marriage. Oddly enough as previously mentioned a local theatre company performed a play which I forget the name of that was so similar to the night we split that likely played in the theatre a year of two after our separation. I cried during the whole play. Not sobbing tears but the quiet tears that stream down one's face. It was eerie that such a play was written.

It was confusing for all of us my so quickly having a boyfriend. My daughters never liked this man. I had been enjoying the attention and having someone with a similar belief system that I initially did not see how unhealthy this relationship was. Another factor was this man having an active alcohol and drug addiction that was not so apparent in the beginning. And when I later discovered he had not paid his taxes (something against my own values) and was about to claim bankruptcy I was questioning myself as to what I was getting into. Perhaps he was just a nudge for my leaving my marriage (or a gale force wind).

I know I have to accept what decisions I have made that does not mean I have to like these decisions. I also know my ex-husband likely regrets some of his choices. Within weeks of our separation we went on a family trip that had been previously planned. We decided to go on this holiday as a separated couple. Initially my husband and I were to stay in two different condos. It ended up we stayed together in one condo each sleeping in different rooms and each having one of our daughters share the room with us. In many ways this was a wonderful vacation. It was like being a family again even grocery shopping together. Yet we were separated. It was at this trip that I went to a healer and she told me I needed to ask my husband to choose me or the alcohol. Prior to the trip we agreed as parents not to discuss our relationship until we returned to Canadian soil. We might have had some resolution had we not made this rule. Once we hit an airport on Canadian soil, though not our home city I asked him this question of choosing alcohol or me. His response was I had no right putting a condition as I was the one that was with someone else. He in my mind/heart chose alcohol. On another occasion he chose me, and I felt it was too late.

We made a few efforts to try and resolve our separation without much luck. It was almost like we both were on opposite pages. When I wanted to try he did not want to try and vis-a-versa. He has questioned his own drinking. At one point he was so afraid after coming home after a houseboat trip with his buddies due to a drinking near fatal accident. He shared in a split second he was driving a house boat and almost crashed into the other house boat coming close to killing people and he blamed this on his "use". Stating this would never have happened if he had been "sober". He wanted to tattoo his hand between the pointer finger and thumb with HBT, for House Boat Tour, as a reminder for what he called his own stupidity. I talked him out of the tattoo thinking he would not have wanted this on his skin. Perhaps I should have not said anything, and it might have helped him. As within a few short weeks he down played this near tragedy and it was minimized to where it was not a big deal.

Having had two parents that never got well from their addictions I did not have a lot of faith in change and I likely was giving him the freedom to live as he wanted to not how I wanted him to. I have been taught by 12th step fellowship that I cannot change another person.

Chapter 8 Self-Reflective Questions:

* Have friends or family encouraged you to leave your marriage? If so what have they said?

* Is there someone else vying for your attention?

* Is there someone else vying for your partner's attention?

* Have you as a married couple addressed this? If so how?

* Would it in your opinion be best to separate/divorce before exploring an outside relationship?

* Would you let your children know of this exploration? If so what age do you think would be appropriate to inform a/the child/children?

* Are your eyes "wide open" in exploring other relationships?

* Have your viewpoints/beliefs grown further apart in your relationship?

* If so is there anything you can do to try and help each of you better understand each other?

CHAPTER 9

Children/Teens and Dating

I have found since being separated my children, now both young adults, have adjusted to my dating in their own ways. We wanted, my ex and I, to continue parenting to the best of our abilities. I must admit at my first leaving I fell short of being the kind of parent that I wanted to be. This might have been partly due to my own difficult time adjusting to the reality of a relationship ending. I never saw myself as someone who would leave a marriage. I brought my boyfriend close to my children too soon. Part of me I think thought well... the marriage is over so might as well move on. A part of me really believed my ex-husband no longer loved me and this would not hurt him. I am so sorry for having done this to him and to my children. I remember the first time my ex met my then boyfriend. It was painful to watch the man I loved for years (and still will love as the father to our children) be gracious about meeting my then new boyfriend. I do a lot of trauma work and I believe this was a traumatic event for my ex and for me. In trauma: time can slow down, and pictures of the event have an uncanny clarity, even now writing this I can see this picture of this event taking place.

The other thing I never really realized is that I would have to literally see my children much less. Previous to our separation I was the primary parent seeing my children daily. Now I did not get to see them when they were at their father's and for sure when he took them on holidays. One of my hardest memories is the first time they went to the lake without me. This had been a usual family trip at Easter. I cried a tonne that Easter and later found out my youngest had done the same and was inconsolable while they were at the lake. Here I thought they would all be fine at the lake and life would go on without me. I had not realized they might be suffering too. For the most part we as parents to our children did our best to try to parent together. It was a new kind of parenting. I may have already mentioned this but one gift out of the "S#@t*" of divorce was my ex stepped up and became a more involved and better dad/father. I think all of us would agree.

It was interesting my oldest did not like her dad dating and made it difficult for him. My youngest made it difficult for me to date. In retrospect I wish I had not subjected them so early to my dating life.

My ex and I both had to accommodate our children in this aspect. I remember a teen client told me about her separated mother and how this mother had her boyfriend over and was openly sexual, as in having a bath with her new partner, and this teen was at home at this time. This teen child was struggling with this sexual openness in her home. I learned from other's experiences that I did not wish to have any of my boyfriends overnight if it was my turn to have the children. They had enough to adjust to without further adding to their stress. One man in particular my one child felt unsafe around. I wish I had paid more attention to this. My daughter's instincts have been good when she has judged people around me. Unfortunately, she still needs to hone this instinct for herself.

Once I was more myself I did try and take their perspectives into my decision making. One man I dated I did not want him to meet my children as I was not even sure how I felt about him. He was told this and I asked him to leave as my child was due home within the hour. He outright refused stating he should get to know her. I ended up shortly thereafter breaking up with him and this was a major factor in my decision.

When we separated our children were 14 and 11. I have been counselling for over 35 years and have learned plenty from my clients and I am constantly learning. I must admit until I went through this myself I was limited in my knowledge of the impact a separation can have. Also, I want to make you the reader aware there are many variables and factors, so you might want to remember your situations will vary. One theme of my child client's (even adult children), that have parents that have separated share with me is their loyalty to their parent(s). For this reason, please do not "bad mouth" their other parent no matter how angry or hurt you may be, at least not in front of the child/teen/adult child. It is one thing for a child to talk ill of their parent(s) it is another to hear you do so. Also, I have seen the child may actually really like whoever you or your partner is dating but they may out of loyalty not admit this in effort to spare their other parent's feelings.

Another factor I have observed is if you date a parent of your child's friend this can further complicate things.

The children may not know how to make this transition of your dating their friend's parent. Children's ages may also be a factor. If the relationship ends it may also end your child's relationship with their friend.

Dating when you have children can prove difficult for all parties involved. I chose not to date someone with younger children as I did not wish to have a parenting role of other children. Though I may have liked some of the men with younger children I chose to opt out before getting involved. This was my personal choice. Others might be excited to have little ones come into their lives. One fellow when meeting him interviewed me as if I was a nanny, not as if he was interested in me personally. This was a red-flag for me. I believe he was busy with his work and was looking for a relationship where the person could also be a co-parent, or thee parent. I have been a nanny and enjoyed this very much as a younger person. I do not wish to raise another person's children at this stage of my life. Keep in mind other's expectations in a dating relationship. There could also be the whole parenting style difference in a blended family or even in a dating couple. I see this in my private practice. Negotiating roles with a new partner and their children is important. A book that I heard was no longer in print; "Cinderella Revisited", the book talked about blended families and how the children's actual parent ought to do the parenting or discipline and the parent's new partner is better to just get to know the child and form a relationship not including discipline. This may also vary due to the age of the children.

Dating introduces many things to consider for a dating couple, especially if there are children involved.

Not to mention non-traditional dating. One book called, "The Ethical Slut, A Practical Guide to Polyamory, Open Relationships and Other Adventures", Dossie Easton and Janet W. Hardy, may give some ideas for couples that are not monogamous in their relationships.

There are also the relationships where one partner may now be ready to admit or are just now discovering that their sexuality is not heterosexual and may now be willing to admit this in the marriage ending. I am aware that in some cases couples split for this reason and they never told their partner that this was a main reason for separating/divorcing.

It is interesting that until my teen found her first love interest she did not like me dating. It was as though she had her own relationship and perhaps could better understand my wanting to have a relationship. This transition took place while I was dating my current partner. Initially she wanted my boyfriend to leave and not get to know him. This all mellowed once she had a boyfriend. It was cute as I listened to her initial comments about my current relationship, her insults of him were mild making me think she didn't really have much negative to say about him. Once she had her own boyfriend she seemed more open to my having a relationship. When I asked her about a year into my new relationship what had changed she shared initially in the beginning of my relationship she was trying to protect my heart. I cherish this comment and know now as a mom that protecting my heart is my job not hers. I get it now as I would love to protect her heart, but this is a large part out of my control and is a huge part of her own growth and awareness. Open communication when a child is ready and being the type of loving adult, they feel is approachable is huge in parenting. This applies if the marriage is intact or if separation occurs.

Watching a dear friend separate and find her new relationships was also a learning for me. Again, her process was different than mine. I do not know if I will marry again as she has. I enjoy the concept of choosing to be with someone daily without the obligation to marry. I currently am not even ready to live with someone. My children are young adults and in University/College. One lives with me the other is in another province though we are in continual contact as she runs into hurdles and joys in her own life.

My daughter that lives with me currently, I do not feel it is fair to bring my partner into her home. I see it as her home too and I want her to feel comfortable and for her to have her own privacy. My oldest initially blamed my not remarrying or living with my partner on my daughter that lives at home. I shared that it is my choice and that I enjoy having my own space and being able to say goodnight and goodbye to my partner at the end of the night. This might change but this is currently how this is. I really don't know much about Goldie Hawn and Kurt Russell, but I am intrigued that for years they were together and not married. I am not sure if they are married now?

I had been at a 50th Wedding Anniversary celebration at a past boyfriend's parents and that couple, his parents, had a dual wedding so the other couple were also there celebrating their 50th, so 100 years between the two couples. The boyfriend I was then dating stated his parent's marriage was horrible in his opinion. The celebration was interesting and yet it too made me question the quality of relationships. Yet it is interesting as part of me still feels somewhat guilty for not fulfilling my wedding vows. The until death do us part vow. I have worked with many couples of domestic violence and abuse that have potentially been guilted into staying in an abusive relationship because of such vows. I do not agree to this either. I have an article written by a priest speaking of many kinds of death in a marriage and it was written to help these couples ease the guilt of separating. The priest spoke of many kinds of death in a marriage.

I do know both of my daughters have made it clear if I should ever remarry they want to be there. This is good for me to know as relationships are more than about just the couple they can be about community. I remember running into a client at a rock concert I was at. I was definitely not in my "counsellor hat", when this young gentleman came up to thank me. I later remembered where and what client he was, though I drew a blank initially because of the location where we saw each other. He pulled out his phone showing me pictures of his children and his wife excited that I had helped them remain as a family. He had been a client in a group of men that I worked with in helping them to stop abusing their partners and teaching healthy relationship skills. This was wonderful to hear the changes that he had made and the impact these contributed to keeping his family. I often do not get to hear the "happy endings" as I often just see people for a specific chunk of time in their lives. It was great to hear such a positive result from earlier counselling. Sometimes changes can save a relationship.

One more story I feel like sharing here. I went to a yoga class instructed by a friend. At the beginning of the class I was on my mat relaxing when I heard someone roll out their mat beside me. When I looked up to see who it was I was surprised to see it was my ex-husband and at the time I spotted him he also saw me. He offered to go to the concurrent class down the hallway. I said no that this should be ok. After class I jokingly commented it had been nice spending time with him in this way. I later told my friend instructing the class about my ex being there. My friend was surprised and stated he knew him for a long time and did not know that that was my ex. I wished my ex would have joined yoga when we had still been together as it might have helped us as his not being calm was a part of our relationship breakdown. That darn hindsight being 20/20! Yet I am happy for him and the changes he is making.

Chapter 9 Self-Reflective Questions:

* Were you from a home where your parents separated/ divorced? If so, do you remember your parent/ parents dating?

* Do you recall how this made you feel?

* If you had siblings do you remember them sharing how your parent's dating made them feel?

* Did you find they did anything that made you feel more comfortable in their dating relationship/s?

* If so what?

* If it made you feel uncomfortable is there anything you wish they had done differently? Is there anything you wish they would have known or been aware of?

* Are there any lessons here for you now?

CHAPTER 10

Grandparents/ Relatives/ Friends

This might be a short chapter, yet I wanted to acknowledge this topic. As I mentioned in the last chapter that others are influenced or impacted by couple relationships. My dear young male friend did not want to talk to me for a time after my separation. I'm only guessing it was due to his own hurt at our relationship, marriage breakup. He had been a part of my relationship from the beginning. He was in my care as a child and he spent time with my boyfriend and I before we were engaged and even played an important part in our wedding ceremony, being our ring bearer. I was surprised by his not wanting to talk to me initially I had not really realized he too would be impacted.

His parents were also impacted. I must say these relationships have been confusing for me as they were like my family and not my family off and on over the years. When my husband and I split we initially agreed for each of us to leave the house a few days alternating so our children initially would be less disrupted. This way our children could stay in the family home, while as parents we alternated. I was almost shocked when my then husband went to stay at the people I just mentioned home, whom I considered as "my" family. My own parents had been deceased for a long time. Even my then husband's parents spoke to me of their being confused why their son did not go to their home as we were all living in the same city. I felt betrayed when the family I saw as my family took my then husband into their home after our separation. This made me feel that I could not go to their family home when it was my turn to leave the house. It further confused me why the lady of this household wondered why I did not confide in her when I felt she had chosen his side. This relationship in my heart has been confusing for a long time.

So perhaps in your familial/ friendship relationships as you knew them, separating will have similar confusion about your relationships with others or about loyalty. I have heard some people feel threatened by single people as if, "it" separation is contagious. I know one of my friends told her husband after my separating that her husband better "behave" or he will be getting his notice. Characteristically speaking I'd like to think just because one-person separates does not mean friends will also separate. It does make sense though to have a check on one's own relationship when you witness someone else's marriage result in a separation.

I've had clients where due to their adult children separating that this has impacted their ability to visit the grandchildren. In some instances, these extended family members and friends have nothing but the best interest of the children in mind. They may also benefit the children by having a stable relationship in place while the parents are contributing instability with the family splitting. Grandparents may feel heartbroken when their grandchildren may not be allowed to visit while a family is in the midst of separating. Some grandparents do a lot of child care, and when a separation occurs this may be disrupted or not allowed.

Sometimes child custody goes to court where visitation is being decided from someone other than the parents. At times there is a large amount of hurt that information may not be "truthful" in the court proceedings and it may be one parent's intention to harm the other parent. I am sure there are circumstances where a parent is a danger to the child and in the case of separation the concerned parent may try to protect their child from the other parent. I am aware other times it is not out of trying to protect the child but rather out of pain or vindictive reasons a parent may try to stop one parent from seeing their children. It may even have to do with jealousy of not wanting their children exposed to their ex's new romantic relationship. The first lesson I learned in law is that: "Law and Justice is not synonymous", meaning just because it is the law does not mean it is fair. I know of false accusations and people not coming from their "higher self" in the dealings they have with others. As mentioned sometimes people separating replace the love for the other with hate.

I know couples that have no children and yet the separation/divorce agreement can take years and thousands of dollars to attempt resolution due to divorcing couples not being able to or wanting to work together. An old movie, "The War of the Roses", 1989, Kathleen Turner and Michael Douglas, depicted this on the big screen. Love and hate can be a fine line.

I have worked with family violence and in one court ruling I witnessed the law not being just. In this particular situation of family violence, a woman was choked to unconsciousness in front of their children by her then husband. Later the court ruled that these children must travel on the bus to visit their father. Not only were these children young, I myself as a mother would not have put my own children unaccompanied by a chaperone on a bus. The safety of these children on the bus and the safety of the abusive other parent's home was in question. I am not convinced that the courts necessarily do what is in the best interest of the children or families.

For the most part my ex-husband and myself have been civil and concerned for our children. I had a compliment from our youngest. She knows friends where parents cannot be in the same room after separation and may be unable to communicate as parents. Because of this lack of communication between some parents that have separated the children are able to tell untruths as to their whereabouts. This inability for separated/divorced parents to communicate can cause some avenue for high risk behaviours by their children. For example, a child may say they are staying at the other parent's house and this may not be true. This can and does happen in intact homes, children lying about their whereabouts. However, she stated because my ex and I for the most part get along and communicate this means her whereabouts was usually known to each of us. She thanked us for this, our knowing where she is. It is just only recently that she is comfortable with us being in the same place at the same time, but there are times she still prefers we are not.

Family and friends may not understand how hard being together after separation/divorce can be at times. Initially there were times as a separated couple we would not always be aware of the impact of us being in the same room at the same time could be. I have tried to let those close to me know that there are times our being at the same event can be difficult and at times this is considered and at other times this is not. As mentioned certain friends that I saw as family invited my ex and his girlfriend to their out of country condo for a vacation. I call this the "tea incident", I share this in hopes of pointing out to extended family and friends that their good intentions may also be seen as hurtful. While my ex was at their condo I asked my ex if he could buy me some of my favourite tea at the nearby grocery store, you cannot buy this tea where I live. His reply was that we do not need to buy gifts for each other anymore...that he would not ask me to pick up something for him while I was on holiday. I asked my boyfriend and he stated this wouldn't bother him to pick something up from where I might be holidaying. Anyway, I was incensed that he would not do this simple favour for me and I felt entitled telling myself he wouldn't even be there without having known me. I swore in my text saying this would not be a gift and I could pay him back. This was not about the tea it was my hurt about him being on holiday where I saw as my parental types lending him their condo. His reply was, "holy...bitter at all?" I was bitter and for the most part this is not my typical nature. I realize family and friends have the "right" to do as they wish it is just that I was hurt by this and I might not have seen it until it came out in my behaviour.

Another hurt by family/friends. When I separated, I mentioned earlier about some past friends that always told me their opinion of my then husband having a drinking problem. It turned out when he was exploring this for himself and he asked their honest opinion and I believe at the time he wanted feedback and yet both denied ever having said such. I could not believe it, they lied. They may have helped him explore his own drinking which at the time he was motivated to do.

Then to further add hurt, this same couple, when they first heard about our separation they felt "sorry" for me and the woman worried about me being lonely. I did not share I had a boyfriend somehow sensing I would be judged. Sure enough, when I said I had a boyfriend she called me some horrible names damaging our relationship to the point where I have ended it. The final straw was not only did they call me horrible names she further added my children would/could be the same. My children were young and how dare she state such horrible descriptions of our children. I am grateful to my ex as he eventually believed this and also stopped their (our children and his) relationship with them as they tried to see our children behind my back, so to speak. These same people had judged us previously in our marriage such as stating my then husband should not have purchased a truck that he needed for work and that I should not have travelled one time when I had opportunity when our daughter was young. Both of these opinions had been uninvited. I have been learning some friends/family are abusive and do not have the right to be in my/our lives. I encourage others to be careful who you allow into your lives.

I wish I felt safe letting some people know how hurtful I find some of their behaviours to be. In one case I did have a different opinion from their opinion and they cut me off from the relationship for a time. I felt this was a way they tried to control me, a kind of emotional blackmail. It was as if I didn't see it their way they couldn't love me. I get the concept of loved ones not wanting to take sides or not agreeing. I would find it helpful if they at least take my "feelings" into consideration. I'm not saying they need to be mean to the other person, it's just that some boundaries or not extending an invite might help assist their loved one (me) during a separation/divorce.

Chapter 10 Self-Reflective Questions:

* Have you judged other people's separation/divorce when you may not have the whole perspective?

* Have you run into situations where others may treat you as if divorce is contagious?

* Are couples no longer inviting you over where once they did?

* What is your view of loved ones supporting familial ties?

* Can you see how inviting both persons might be difficult for those separated/divorced?

* Have you thought about how this might make you feel if you were in the same shoes?

* Can you see that there might be exceptions where inviting both might make sense? This might include occasions where it is the separating couples children's, Birthdays, Weddings, Grandparents Funerals.

* Can you see there might be exceptions when having both invited may prove hurtful?

* Do you think it is ok to ask family/friends to not invite you both at the same time?

* Do you think you have the right to know that the other person has been invited?

* Have you taken into consideration how the new partner/s, new relationship may feel or be impacted by their partner's ex being at the event?

* Have you considered how the divorce couple's children/teens/adult children might be impacted by the various ex's and their new/current partners being invited to the same event?

* What boundaries might you consider helpful?

Pets and Divorce

In our relationship when I was first dating my husband to be I had a dog, a shelty cross – a Heinz 57 (a dog of an uncertain breed). She appeared to be part miniature collie and dachshund (wiener dog). My boyfriend had never had an indoor dog as he lived on a farm. He was great with my dog even taking her for long bike ride runs. And when she eventually died he was mournful, and this too showed me the love this man was capable of.

In our marriage we had two yellow lab dogs. The first was the dominant dog in his litter. We were advised to get help with this puppy's training which we did. In our training to manage our dog it was very much about learning about a "pack" mentality. I had to learn to deepen my voice for training our dog. We were told that when my husband came home he should kiss me first and then give affection to the dog. That we were to eat before feeding the dog so that he could learn his "place". In addition, I was pregnant with our first child and so we learned some preventative things in training our dog to be better with children. Things like teaching him to only play with his toys and not other toys. In addition to giving his food and taking it away and giving it back so he would be less protective of his food around children. This dog ended up being a great love of ours. Friends that normally were afraid of dogs were comfortable with him.

Our second dog was also a lab, we got him near the end of our first dog's life hoping he would help train the pup. This also helped us when our oldest dog died to have another beloved animal around. The puppy was more a dog for our daughters and he was also trained as a bird hunting dog for my husband. When we separated I was the one that left the household. There were pros and cons to this and I hope to address partly the pros and cons of keeping the main residence after a separation/ divorce in another chapter. Since I left the house I did not have a place for the dog. Thus, the dog remained part of their household.

When my ex got a new job his job required more travel and my eldest had moved away. He would expect our youngest to look after the dog and often this would be at my house. The marital home had been outfitted with a kennel and fenced yard which was more dog friendly. I have wood floors (pine so a softer wood). Having the dog over with his long sharp nails and even if his nails were trimmed he damaged my floors. I could not let him upstairs at my place as I have an office where I see clients, and some clients have allergies. The dog visited, he did not live with us (my youngest and I). I found having the dog a bit of an intrusion. If you've ever had a water dog, they have an oil in their hide that repels water which can have a smell and because he was more an outdoor dog he would arrive pungent. I asked my ex if he could wash the dog before he came to my place. He suggested I can do it. I felt this was rude and my initial request was ignored. I did end up bathing the dog when he came. Summer bathing a dog is fine but bathing a large dog in winter or cold weather was a bit of a challenge (easier now that there are dog washes similar to a car wash). The next time the dog came my daughter took him to a dog wash place.

In another family where their relationship broke down. The lady in that relationship would allow the ex-partner to visit their mutual dogs only if her ex would pay to have the dogs groomed. This was not a shared expense and I felt this was not fair to the man. Grooming of two small dogs was expensive! Perhaps these are things that need to be in a separation agreement we never spoke of this when we were separating.

I have since built a kennel out of pallets and chicken wire for our dog but he always wanted to escape. As mentioned at the original home he has a proper heavy duty kennel. Once when he visited he got away and I found him being led around the neighbourhood on a leash by another couple and I claimed him and thanked them for keeping him safe. Now our dog does not come visit, my daughter is older and drives so now she cares for him at her father's home. Our dog has a congenital eye problem and is now blind, I believe it is best for him to stay at my ex's as it is better set up for him and he knows the lay out better.

My daughter wants me to get a smaller house dog and I understand the value of a new family member. I also understand it is a long-term commitment as my dogs have all lived 14 years or so. I am at a phase where I may wish to do more travel. My daughter states she would look after a new dog, but she is still in University and it is too uncertain to know after convocation where she will be. She is studying Education and often first year teachers must accept teaching positions in rural communities. In addition my own experience of being a pet owner as a university student, it was a challenge to find a place.

There are lots of articles on the healing benefit of animals, but each family needs to know if they are prepared for this kind of a commitment.

It's kind of funny as when I was going steady with my boyfriend that became my husband I was trying to find a home for my dog as renting with pets is difficult. I placed an ad in the local paper stating that I was looking for a new home for a beloved pet. I received a phone call from a stranger stating it sounded like I did not want to give up my pet. I agreed and shared I was a university student and could not find a place to rent that allowed pets. This caller told me he might have a solution for me. He went on to say he has a duplex and that perhaps he could strike a deal with me if I would do some yard work. I grew excited. Then he said the only thing is that they share a yard and that they are nudists. I said that shouldn't be a problem, I would not go out to the yard if they were there. He said no actually they would want me to be out there, as they were exhibitionists. This phone call surprised me, and I no longer felt comfortable looking for a new home for my dog.

I then came up with the solution to move in with my boyfriend to help keep my dog, as my boyfriend's landlord has a dog and I asked if he could ask his landlord if he could have a dog suggesting we could move in with him. It turned out this is just what we did. I'm not saying I was ready for a live-in relationship, I was more looking into finding a home for my dog and I. My boyfriend ended up being one of the best roommates I ever had, and the dog situation was resolved. I guess I could have asked my boyfriend to let my dog live with him and I could have lived elsewhere. Unfortunately, I had not realized the position I put my boyfriend in. His father was of a religion that forbid living together before marriage. His father as I may have already mentioned wrote biblical referenced letters scolding us for, "living in sin". We were eventually engaged and married which stopped the letters, but this was not our motive for being married. I believe we genuinely loved each other. We were engaged a year after we met and married the following summer.

Chapter 11 Self-Reflective Questions:

* Do you have family pets?

* What did you do to accommodate the animals living arrangements?

* Were the arrangements mutually agreed upon?

* How have the arrangements worked out?

* Are you aware of how your ex feels about the arrangements?

* Were children a factor when deciding upon pet placement?

* Knowing what you know now is there anything you would have done differently?

* Do you have any recommendations for other separating/ divorced families in regards to pet placement/sharing?

* If your ex and children add animals to their household do you think you should help in the care of these new pets?

Keeping the Marital Home: Pros/Cons

Whether or not to keep the marital home was something I never gave a lot of thought to. I know some books on separation and divorce must talk about this as I have had friends state they have read about how it is recommended to keep the family home. I never loved the last home we were living in. My dream home had been the one prior to that one. We decided to move back to the city after being away for 15 years due to work. As already mentioned I was promised a job in the city and this fell by the way side. When we as a family moved back to the city it was then I discovered I no longer had a job, the job I just mentioned. My then husband and I had both been counting on this job. The move back to the city was more stressful as my husband had already quit his position prior to our move. I then found a job that was not what I wanted nor in my field to make sure bills were paid. Eventually I went back into Private Practice.

The stress of finances hurt our marital relationship. My parents had both been alcoholic and terrible with money. That was back in the day when there were answering machines and my parents would not answer the phone and I would hear bill collectors leaving threatening messages.

Likely as a result of my parents fighting about money, doing bills with my husband would often be fear based for me. This coupled with our different Circadian rhythms. He was a morning person and I was a night owl. His wanting to discuss money in the morning was more difficult than I realized. Luckily, I have since found some better coping strategies with this. I have always been good with money; however, witnessing my parents losing everything I believe has me leaning towards being frugal with my finances.

Our rural home did not sell for a year, so our employment and financial situation was compounded. We had a mortgage and rent to pay. We are fortunate that our in-laws wanted to move into a condo as they did not want the yard work and they helped us out by selling us their home. Their home was to be temporary. I asked/told my husband I needed more sunlight and the rural home we had left had tons of sunlight. Even my mother-in-law felt their home was not to be our home for the long run. My husband I think was fine with the home. It had no sentimental meaning to him as his parents had only been there for about 5 years. I think he thought it was all about "money" but to me it was an environment I wanted to improve on for my own "peace of mind", I believe I suffer SAD (Seasonal Affective Disorder) where sunlight helps alleviate this condition.

Since the home we were living in at the time of our separation was not a home I felt attached to, I felt he wanted the home more than I did. I did not want to keep the family home. I now realize the children felt a kinship to the house as it had been their grandparent's home and our home. It was in a neighbourhood where they had friends and their school.

Initially in our separation I home sat for a girlfriend's

parents while they were out of Canada I am sure as a favour for me and a favour for them to help sell their house. Only one daughter stayed with me, the other was too hurt I believe.

I eventually rented nearby their dad's home and their school, so they would often come to my place for lunch. If they stayed and forgot anything as in terms of personal belongings or school homework it was only a few blocks away and easy to get.

When I looked at purchasing a home I could get more "bang for my buck" so to speak in the area I chose to buy in. In our original neighbourhood the housing was older and most needed updating.

In my newer neighbourhood things would likely last longer needing less renovations.

Somewhere I had read don't buy in the neighbourhood where your children go to school as this will change as they graduate. The place I chose to buy was across town from their home and it turned out to be a difficult adjustment for my children. The inconvenience of having to drive across town if they wanted something from their other home was difficult, especially in winter. It became easier once my children were in high school and had their own driver's license(s). One semester of high school one of my daughters tried a semester at a high school in my area. It ended up being less than ideal as it appeared students were not as welcoming, so she returned to her original school. Once one of my daughters attended our local University it turned out the bus route was a bit easier from my location.

I had thought when my daughters first saw my "our" (my daughters' and my) new home I thought they would be pleased. Instead there were tears and terror. I believe the new home signified the true end of a family and now that family was truly split into two homes. I was a bit heartbroken myself and had hoped it would instead signal a new beginning. I had not been prepared for their initial hatred for my new home. Fortunately, I knew more was going on than a dislike of the house.

I was also terrified of being the sole person purchasing the home and I am happy to say so far so good, I have been able to make every payment and even a few extra.

I likely could have received some kind of spousal allowance and partial child maintenance from their father. A friend of mine who is a lawyer stated there are charts for assessing spousal and child support and he thought I would qualify. I believe the lawyer I did use did a poor job of helping me understand this. This might be something you the reader might wish to check into. I also had pride wanting to be self-sufficient. I might have prevented the lawyer from explaining the options to me, plus her daughter had been in an accident and was hurt at the time so this might also have been a factor. Fortunately, my ex as our children's father agreed informally to help with expenses such as Grad, dental, their cars etc. He continues to be an active part of their lives and I am grateful for this.

I believe my brother gave more than his share when he left his wife. The guilt for him I believe was a factor and he I believe gave his ex and his son the house. I have seen people be so bitter about money that the lawyers get so much more than what a peaceful agreement could have been. I did get half of the value of the house and this is what I needed to be financially able to move forward.

I don't know if the adjustment would have been easier for our children if me, "mom" stayed in the family home, I think it could have helped. I might not have been as motivated to move into a home and neighbourhood that suits my peace of mind if I had stayed. In about 3 more years I will likely be an empty nester. I may then move myself, I'm not sure. For now, my home serves the purpose as a nice place to live. Currently my youngest lives with me. As mentioned my oldest lives out of province. They can still stay at their dad's. My oldest had shared she is sad her room at her dad's place is gone due to his downsizing, yet she is always welcome there. Currently both of my girls have their rooms at my place. I am a person that home is an important place.

I am loving my home and my yard and walking in my neighbourhood. The full spectrum of sunlight is also a huge blessing for me living in a place with long winters often six months of the year.

I have had a few clients that wanted to leave everything including the home to the spouse/partner more because they, the client, felt depressed and defeated. I have encouraged them to request half of the property as they may regret not insisting on what is rightfully theirs. Once they are less depressed they can better see the wisdom in this. It helps for them to begin again. Each case may need to be assessed, I do not believe in being a martyr. I am a big believer in self-care and that for parents taking care of yourself and your basic needs leaves less stress on the children. In the same light this will make it easier to take care of your family.

Chapter 12 Self-Reflective Questions:

* Do you have attachment to the home you as a family lived in?

* Do the children have attachment to the place where the family lived?

* Can you afford to keep the family home?

* If so do you want to have the family home?

* Is it possible you want a new start and perhaps a new living location?

* Please consider if you get involved in a new relationship it may be beneficial to have your own place for you and your children.

* If you are single and do not have children it may be important you have your own place.

* In my experience as a counsellor there can be cons to moving in too quickly with another person whether they have children or not. Also cohabit laws may reflect that if you separate the other person may be entitled to owning property.

* My girlfriend that divorced before me kept her place when she moved in with her new partner out of wanting, "a back-up plan". When they did get married they kept both places for a while.

   They eventually sold one and payed off her place and bought a new place together. Throughout they had a prenup (prenuptial agreement: a before marriage legal agreement) and changed this to a postnup (postnuptial agreement: an after marriage legal agreement). A main concern is she wanted her children to have an inheritance from her hard work and did not want this to go to his adult children and wanted the same for her husband and his children. As it turned out my friend did predecease her spouse. They both spoke to me of the importance of a prenup before her death.

* In my work I have talked to another client that did not have children, but he unfortunately found his prenup did not hold up from a different province so please check into this for yourself.

* In my work I do not think it is healthy for partners after separating to live together in the same home. I know of some instances where this occurs and I believe this is detrimental. My guess is that this may have to do with expenses; however, living together after divorce can have a huge cost on mental, physical and spiritual health. I have witnessed the negative impact this has had on the children as well.

Holidays – Easter

In Grief there are different seasons. Some are harder to bare than others. Easter was known as our family time to go to the lake and stay at a cabin.

When I was a University student I had been a nanny to 3 boys and responsible for taking the boys to their family cabin for fun. As a result, I was treated as family and saw their cabin as part of my place too. My husband became a part of going to the lake. He and the father to these boys were a good match and enjoyed activities together. Once we had our own children we would often go to the lake for Easter and a high light was making Pysanka with the girls. There was always an Easter surprise of chocolate and an Easter egg hunt. I found after the Separation/ Divorce having holidays felt like a loss of family. The first Easter my girls and their father went to the lake without me and with this family and I was not invited. I believe as a result I had been physically sick, the throwing up type. I wondered if it was emotional as in "not being able to digest our marriage being over, and the end of family as we knew it." (Louise Hay, "You Can Heal Your Life"). I also did not understand why my ex had the privilege of using the cabin.

I later found out our youngest though excited about going to the lake cried most of the weekend because her mother, I, had not been there. I too did my fair share of crying. This was not the only Easter I struggled with. I think now things have gotten better and more "normalized", whatever that means. Perhaps we simply became used to the loss of traditions. I think a huge part is still missing the comfort of having a family. In my mind our family had consisted of: a dad, a mom, two kids and a dog. I realize today there are many kinds of families. I am redefining what family looks like in my situation.

I know my daughters are growing up and one has moved out of province and we will not all be able to get together for the holidays. My mother made things special many years around holidays and I enjoy having holiday traditions. This morning talking to my daughter on the phone she stated she misses us. I told her I miss her too. Yet currently we do not live near each other and at this time it is hard to know if holidays will include each other, at least by phone it will. So even without divorce, family traditions and times together may change if family members move to distant locations. I remember as a married couple we had lived out of country for a year in a different culture and we had to decide how we wished to celebrate our Canadian traditions when we were abroad. It was also an opportunity to experience the country's traditions and festivals that we were visiting (Japan). Discovering and creating new traditions could be a goal for each family if they see this as important.

Chapter 13 Self-Reflection Questions:

*   What family traditions have you had with your spouse?

*   Did you blend each of your family of origin traditions?

*   Grief is about loss, sometimes the loss or grief is about losing traditions. Traditions often hold a family or culture together.

*   For myself after separation/divorce I did not initially wish to "celebrate" certain holidays or traditions. Christmas was a main event that I had heartache over. Is there a holiday that is more difficult for you?

*   Is there a new tradition you might wish to start with your new life? What might that be?

     I know for years after the loss of my mother whenever I made our Valentines Cookies it was bittersweet. In fact, some years I made so many that I would be exhausted, and I needed to learn moderation. Are some traditions now difficult for you?

*   Remember you are entitled to your feelings.

CHAPTER 14

Pining for my Ex

No one told me 7 years after our separation/Divorce that I would still at times be missing my Ex. It currently is 9 ½ years and I believe I am finally in acceptance mode and see that we have both moved on. Again, this is part of missing "Our family" and trying to not "should" on myself for not succeeding in making "it" work. We were married, together 25 years and there were many beautiful things about our relationship and family. I still see in my mind's eye my oldest at about 3 years old in a pink skirt and jeweled crown dancing in the living room with her daddy. Walks together. Going to another friend's cabin. I am nostalgic, and it appears I have a larger share of nostalgia than some. I have many keep sakes that I have attached personal memories to. I took a class in my initial separation that was supposed to help heal a person experiencing separation/divorce and I will not mention the organization's name as I found it not at all helpful. One thing I did find at the time is that out of 10 or so members in the class I was the only one that could admittedly state that I still loved my ex and that I knew I needed to move on. I will likely always have love for him. I also know I need to let him go and continue on in creating a new life for myself.

The irony is that I do have a wonderful new man and he treats me with such kindness and yet at times I miss my ex. This sometimes makes me feel crazy as if something is wrong with me and I ask myself why do I struggle to move on? I have had other clients I have worked with that share this same issue.

Yet others appear to move forward without ever having to look back.

One of my favourite card and meditation books is, "Tao Oracle" by Ma Deva Padma, page 144 – states:

"Consider what it would be like to live with the people and things that help you to feel good about yourself. Then consider the extent to which you are willing to go to make that a reality."

This quote has a deep meaning for me. I now cannot imagine living with someone who does not treat me well. In my early relationship with my ex, he was one of my biggest fans and we would celebrate together. Near the end of our relationship he was so miserable, and I was often the one that was exposed to his miserable moods.

The same book, page 169 -

"letting go makes it possible to energetically move on. The choice of migrating geese to fly south is not really a choice. It is common sense to submit to the changing seasons in pursuit of a more accommodating climate – especially when the alternative would be dangerous. Only humans are so foolish as to ignore the signs, preferring to hold fast even to that which is likely to make them suffer."

It got to the point that I was afraid if I stayed I would not thrive. I had this same decision to make when I moved out of my alcoholic parent's home, the home was toxic, and I had what they called survivors guilt. This time in my unhealthy marriage I had two others to consider. I wanted them to have a chance to be in a healthier home environment. I was naive to think leaving would be easier than it was. We all suffered at the break up of our family. I do believe adjustments have been made and we are in a healthier environment. I believe even my ex and my daughters would agree since my leaving my ex that he has become a healthier father. It is just too bad this couldn't seem to occur within our marriage.

The class I mentioned that I did not find useful had one piece of information I did find helpful. They said for every 5 years in a relationship it takes about a year of healing. We are past 5 years and still are healing and learning. Perhaps like grief it is an ongoing process. With grief there can be many triggers. Losing my mother, I had delayed grief. When I had my own first daughter I revisited the grief of not having my own mother even though it was a happy occasion having our child after many years of infertility. Neither of my parents met our daughters. I would not have wanted my children to have been exposed to my unhealthy parents. I would very much have enjoyed my daughters meeting my parents when they were healthy.

Chapter 14 Self-Reflection Questions:

*   Are you having a difficult time of letting your ex go?

*   Are you finding it difficult to adjust to your family being apart?

*   Is there someone you can talk to that seems to understand what you are adjusting to?

*   Journaling can be helpful.

*   Some counsellors can be helpful.

*   If you did the leaving do you recall your why?

*   If you were left can you see any gifts in the separation/ divorce?

*   Your self-worth is not up to someone else to judge.

*   "Never lose yourself in an attempt to hold on to someone who didn't care about losing you." -Keanu Reeves

*   "You have to learn to get up from the table when love is no longer being served."-Nina Simone

CHAPTER 15

Holidays – Christmas and other Triggers

I have been finding writing this book at times is cathartic and other times it makes me melancholy. Writing this book is a goal I have set so I will try and persevere. The first three or so Christmases after our separation and divorce were horrible. The first we had not planned the timing and essentially broke up just prior to Christmas. I remember some of this vaguely. We sat our daughters down and told them we were separating and the tears from our girls I remember and we as parents tried to be stoic. I honestly don't remember much about that time.

Some of the sequences of Christmas were a blur. I think the first Christmas following our divorce I had invited a girlfriend and her daughters to join us (my daughters and I) for Christmas. She cancelled last minute via a text message. I was particularly hurt and called her to state how hurtful this was and how cancelling via a text was just not ok. We worked it out. I later found out she had some of her own major concerns at the time and had not wanted to share them with me.

Weirdly enough when my ex had our daughters at Christmas I was lonely for them and this "messed with my head", as I had never had to share my girls before. I was invited to a friend's mother's for Christmas and this was appreciated but also bizarre.

I believe the next one, it might have been the third Christmas? We as parents bought our daughters gifts together and though it was not pre planned my ex showed up Christmas morning in order to gift these presents together. We had purchased each daughter a computer, so it was kind of a big gift for us, so we went into the purchase together. My daughters had stayed the night at my place, so we were in my home and it was nice to be together and that their father joined us in the morning, but it was also confusing. I had not realized he was coming. The girls and I were in our PJ's and it felt like being a family, yet we were no longer a family and this was difficult for all of us I believe. I cried when he left. Christmas had been positive as a family prior to our separation. I missed his family, mostly his mother. My "family", that I became a part of after being a nanny wanted to invite my ex to our usual Christmas Eve and I just found it too much and I told them so. They appeared to not understand this as a nephew that was divorced always invited his ex-wife to these events.

How one feels will likely be different for each individual. I remember we used to help a friend as a family, (my daughters, my ex and I) with a fundraiser. The first year after our separation my ex and I both agreed to help. We were told we would sit at the same table for dinner. I think we both thought this should not be an issue. I can only speak for myself, but this was much harder than I anticipated. People at our table assumed we were together, and we never corrected them. My being able to even use the words separated, divorced and my ex have never come easily to me. On the other spectrum going from boyfriend to fiancé and then husband was a challenge as well. I felt though the fundraiser was positive I still felt out of sorts and lost.

I still enjoy having opportunity to visit with my ex. I also still find it difficult. I have by no means mastered this moving forward part of divorce. Our youngest graduated from grade 12 a few years ago. As parents we agreed to not have our respective partners attend. I had shared this with our daughter and she was grateful. This helped me as well by just removing an element that could have been more difficult. For grad day we as a family went to the country side to take pictures. They turned out beautiful. As did my oldest daughter's grad photos when she graduated. Our girls I believe will be glad to have pictures of both parents in them.

The grad supper was nice and we all were respectful of each other. I stayed for the dance as the others left. It would have been nice to have my new partner there, yet this was not my day it was our daughter's. I was grateful to be able to dance with my daughter. I was told by my daughter that other friends divorced parents were not able to sit at the same table. I do not judge these people, I am just grateful that we were able to provide a safe family environment for these occasions.

I work with a lot of clients in the area of trauma and grief. I truly enjoy this type of work, helping people through difficult situations. Part of this work is helping people to be forewarned or aware and even prepared for triggers related to the trauma. I would say being separated and divorced has very much fit the definition of trauma for me. Trauma is not an event, just like grief, trauma is a process.

Some triggers or things that may reopen the wound as one moves forward can be multifaceted. Using a diamond as an example, beauty can come from being under pressure. Pressure can be unbearable at times.

I am quite skilled at trying to find the "gift" in the "sh$%", or the, "silver lining", so to speak.

Triggers happen partly because we are not always aware of how things may impact us. When I first lost my mother, she died a year before I was married, things like wanting to ask for a recipe and realizing as I'd pick up the phone to call her that she was no longer alive was a trigger or a reminder of my loss. Once a few years later I had written out a check to pay for groceries. (I don't think you can even do that anymore.) Following writing the check I felt down and I could not "put my finger on why"? I felt so bad I ended up cancelling a group therapy session I was to lead that evening. Eventually I realized that writing that check had triggered my grief as writing the date I had not realized until much later it was my mother's death date and even through my unawareness writing the check date subconsciously triggered my grief. Once I became conscious of the date my feelings made sense to me. Once I acknowledged the date having written it and what it meant I was able to understand why I was feeling as I was feeling and soon after I felt better.

Triggers can appear as: Look-a-likes, hearing someone with a similar voice, a perfume or cologne, a location, a mutual connection, place or person, a pet or similar breed, a song, a season and any number of things. Often the firsts also contribute to grief, 1st Christmas, 1st Easter, 1st Mother's Day etc.

Other triggers for me are as simple as cooking, in particular making family recipes. Making my mother's Valentine cookies and my mother in law's relish are sure fire triggers for me. They bring happiness and sometimes also the bitter sweet of missing the person the event reminds me of.

I've known clients that go out of their way to avoid triggers. I understand the desire to not want to be reminded of the hurt. Some self-medicate to avoid as well. At some point facing the situation may be what is necessary to move forward. Acceptance does not mean having to like something it is more addressing reality. One therapy I enjoy is Reality Therapy (RT) part of this therapy is known as reframing, a technique where one tries to see the situation in a new framework – the "finding the silver lining", so to speak. An example could be making a favorite recipe and seeing it in its new situation or in a new event or with a new audience and making new memories. Research also shows if you breathe or attempt to remain calm as you remember the event, healing occurs in the part of the brain where the memory is stored. This also eases anxiety, creating or linking new emotion to the memory.

Some people will drive miles/kilometres out of their way to avoid where a fatal accident has taken place. Part of recovery might be facing a past harm or location and placing a new perspective or making peace with the location or being calm in the environment to be better able to cope.

As just mentioned recent trauma work states if you can hold a traumatic memory in a calm, "frame of mind" or calm body state the brain can have healing. This does not mean to put yourself in danger, or visiting someone who has previously been abusive.

Forgiving does not necessarily mean forgetting. I don't believe I need to befriend someone that has hurt me. I might just need to let it go and move forward and to try not to repeat the same mistakes. I work with many types of clients with various issues. One client group would be called, Codependents. As I've mentioned before we are more than our labels. This particular label refers to people that have been hurt in relationships and perhaps tend to repeat unhealthy patterns. Often Codependents work harder or makes more attempts towards the other person's recovery than the person who is unwell. At the same time the Codependent tends to ignore their own wellness or self-care. They tend to be other focused often forgetting their own needs. My counselling teaches me that unless we learn healthier patterns we are destined to repeat unhealthy patterns and unhealthy relationships. I am hoping my own continual self work will help me to have healthier relationships in all areas of my life.

I had a friend that suffered abuse of a husband. Leaving this relationship was very difficult for her. When she moved cities, she had a string of unhealthy employers. She would call in tears telling me how this must be her fault as she was the common denominator. My response was that now that she knows what healthy is she has a low tolerance for abuse of any kind. She applied one more time and fortunately found an employer that treated her right and valued her. Healthy relationships are not just marital ones.

Sometimes people expect the same negative behaviours when a loved one has changed. If the person has changed, loved ones may need to develop patience while they may wonder if the change is for real. People question if change is real and may get angry out of their fear at the person that has said they have changed. It is good for those doing the changing and for their loved ones to be aware of this relationship dynamic.

When I work with addicts in recovery, I tell the addicts to be prepared for loved ones to be on guard around them. I also remind the loved one's to try and not watch their addict's every move, not to smell their breath or to check their eyes. The addict's job is to work on their addiction recovery. The loved one, or Codependent's job is to work on their own personal recovery. "Actions do speak louder than words", pay attention to what one does and not just what one promises. Similarly, I was taught never threaten to leave unless you are prepared to leave, as the behavior needs to emphasise what you said you would do. You won't be believed if you don't follow through.

I find with my new relationship I sometimes expect the same reactions as I have received in previous relationships. I am always pleasantly surprised and grateful that my current partner is kind and patient, a true gift.

Chapter 15 Self-Reflection Questions:

* Can you see that you may still be grieving this past relationship?

* Are there things you need to do to help you cope better?

* Are you aware of your boundaries?

* What other people think may not work for you, listen to your own voice/feelings/guts.

* Can you reframe or see something new as you move forward?

* Do you have "a picture" of how you might like to spend your holiday? Are there a few things you can do this season that might meet part of this "picture"?

* Can you allow yourself to have your feelings and see them as neither good nor bad but just as feelings?

* What self-care things can you practice at this time?

*   If your friend was hurting, what might you do for them? Can you do something you might do for a friend for yourself?

*   Is there someone you can confide in if this is proving difficult?

*   Is there something you can do for someone else? This might help you to see outside of your own situation.

CHAPTER 16

Self-Delusion or Hope

I have heard the saying Denial is not a river in Egypt (sounds like the Nile). Denial can be seen as two-fold. Denial can be seen as hope as in I hope it is not true, or as not seeing what is there or seeing what is there and justifying or making excuses. For example, not seeing someone's poor treatment of you and making excuses for it. I try to have plenty of empathy and would try and put myself into the other person's shoes in effort to imagine what could possibly make someone act so mean or behave in an unkind way. I would make excuses or try to explain the bad behaviour away stating perhaps they are tired or overworked or just having a bad day. One of my favourite counselling acronyms is **HALT** – **H**ungry **A**ngry **L**onely and **T**ired. I have seen these things in myself and my own mood. I try to teach clients to **HALT** or slow down if they are <u>H</u>ungry, <u>A</u>ngry, <u>L</u>onely or <u>T</u>ired. Suggesting if possible if they get HANGRY (Anger due to hunger) that they keep snacks or try and eat something to help correct their blood sugar. I remember reading a study at one time that suggested many family fights (Domestic Violence) occurred at meal times and the study stated because at this time people were hungry. The article suggested having food out prior to a meal to help people not to get grumpy. They suggested carrot and celery sticks so if children filled up on this it would be at least a healthy snack.

I have one child where I believe this was a necessity. As a young mom when I had to grab groceries after a long day I would go and grab a box of crackers off the store shelf and open it, so my kids had something to nibble on which made grocery shopping that much easier. This also applies to adults I remember in one of my pregnancies I was also working in the schools. I went to different schools and one time I felt, "I stole" an apple out of the staff fridge. I say I stole it because I had no idea whose it was. I also felt desperate as if I had not eaten something I feared I would be grumpy with my next client, and I was working with children, so I knew I needed to be in a good frame of mind.

Angry, if one is angry it is best to cool or calm down so halt also applies here. Studies about Fight and Flight (also known as the acute stress response) now we also add Freeze during this natural physiological survival response. During this response the mammalian brain is in charge (the sympathetic nervous system). The frontal lobe or the central cortex is not working during this response and so rational thought is lacking during a survival response. If a person is in a survival response it is advised if in no imminent danger, they halt or take some time to calm so they can re-engage their rational thought. They can do this by self calming via the parasympathetic system, this gives a chance for the rational part of the brain to be back in use. The parasympathetic reset can take 20-60 minutes for the body to return to its pre-arousal state. Once calm the rational part of the brain is re-engaged.

It is also important to note a perceived threat is treated like a real threat to the body/mind so if one imagines danger a fight flight response can also occur.

In simpler terms if one is angry it is important to cool down so one can act more rationally.

I have taught many people about the Fight Flight response (fight-or-flight response was first described in the 1920's by American physiologist Walter Cannon; referencing the article by Kendra Cherry, March 1, 2018 from the site: "Verywell mind"). When couples are fighting for example, one or both may be in the survival response, in the non rational state and one may follow the other around wanting some answers or to keep the conversation or fight going. I try to teach the couple they need to give the other person space, by letting the other person walk away or for themselves to walk away. It is best that prior to an argument the couple set up a rule or agreement to not follow the other, rather to give space, for approximately an hour in order for the other or both to be able to calm down before coming back to the 'hot' topic. Otherwise if one cannot flee they will then engage in the fight, aka the fight or flight response. Giving someone a chance to flight may prevent a fight. Many people have fear of abandonment and may find it difficult to allow their partner or child to leave a room. Preparing clients to know ahead about the departure will help calm the fear of abandonment. It is important for clients to agree to meet back after a period of calming down. One couple I knew, prior to understanding this dynamic, one partner would purposely play on their partner's fear of abandonment by fleeing the scene and purposely staying away unannounced to add further injury to their partner. Touching base even by phone after a fight is recommended. It is important to take time after a cooling off period to address the issue/s in an effort to attempt to resolve issues rather than to just bury them.

<u>L</u>onely in HA<u>L</u>T speaks to the times when someone feels lonely. Sometimes people feel lonely even in a crowd. It is suggested they need to find someone to talk with or reach out to. I used to love the commercials where a child was sad and reached out to the family pet, that could work too. You might have a good person that may help you feel less alone or heard. If you don't want advice you can always let the person know this, as sometimes people think you are coming to them to problem solve, and not just to share and sort.

Lastly for this acronym we have <u>T</u>ired in HAL<u>T</u>. I know if I am tired its way easier to be frustrated so halting here is also good. Sometimes a walk around the block is as helpful as a nap. When I am tired I try to be gentle with myself and not to do difficult tasks if I can put them to another time when I have more energy. I remember when we had our second child and how tired we (their father and I) both were. I could no longer rest with a toddler when our baby had a nap and it was a whole other level of fatigue. Just bundling two opposed to one to head out in the winter was an adjustment. At one time I had put a pizza on the roof of the car and drove away leaving it up there due to my exhaustion fog. Take heed of the HALT and take really good self-care when you are tired.

I have this insight and when others are potentially hungry, angry, lonely or tired I give them more leeway for what I would describe as bad behaviour. What I've had to learn is to not accept bad behaviour though still having empathy. I now try and hold others accountable and not take on the responsibility of their poor behavioural choices. After our divorce my ex told me he wished I would have fought with him more. I do not like to fight. He made it sound like if I had been meaner he would have behaved better. I find fault in this ill logic. I reason if I am nice the other person may feel safer and may then choose better actions or behaviour. I do not agree that my being nice encouraged bad or negative behaviour. He is responsible for his own actions/behaviour.

I remember in our early days I stated I do not want spanking of our children in our home. I felt harming a child does not actually help a child to do better, I preferred compassion and explanation. Initially he argued he was corporally punished. I asked how that had worked? I asked if he corrected his behaviour or if he would get angry and just try not to get caught. He agreed the latter was likely true. I will always be grateful to my Developmental Psychology professor (I believe his name was Professor Farthing), he emphasized children are people and need to be treated as such. I believe it is referred to as the golden rule: treat others as you wish to be treated. Barbara Colorosso (one of her books is, "Kids Are Worth It") I have heard her speak in person on two occasions and she emphasis this point. Current information shares that if a child is emotionally overwhelmed, we do more good assisting them by remaining calm and not further adding to their overwhelm. We are the adults and it is our role to role model calmness and capability.

My own mother (though she was an unwell woman later in life) treated my brother and I with the utmost respect. As a result, I tried to respect her even when I was out of her site. I tried to be a responsible child/teen out of respect to her. I must confess I was harsh on my father who was also unwell and he was unbelievably harsh on us. Once I learned to see him as a "sick" person I no longer treated him badly rather I learned to transfer my hate to his disease and not to him as a person.

I think my having hope is one of the reasons I stayed so long in an unhealthy relationship. Hope is the other side of denial. Rather than deny - one hopes it's not true or that things can get better. I always hoped he would be kinder as I had/have faith in his potential. I also see others as having the integrity of their own choices and consequences. It was and has been a huge sadness having our marriage dissolve. I have been actively working on redefining family and what that means to me.

I used to beg my mother to leave my father and that was a different time when couples did not divorce in numbers as we do today. I was talking to a friend from high school and we could only think of one friend that had divorced parents then and now it is difficult for my children when they were in high school to think of those that have intact families. This book is not about statistics, so I think I'll leave that there.

Looking back, I now can see the love my mother had for my father. At the time I could not see or entertain this concept of her loving him. People stay for a number of reasons. I do believe, though this is not necessarily a fact, that my mother died young as a result of being in such an unhealthy marriage. I've had clients that stay in unhealthy relationships. For the most part I let people get to their decision on their own. There are times I have shared with clients the negative impact their marriage has on them and I find it partly understandable why they stay. Leaving is not easy. Leaving my marriage was the hardest thing I believe I have ever done. Leaving is not the cowards way. For me leaving was brave and took plenty of courage both financially, spiritually and energetically. Divorce is not for the faint of heart. I have worked with men and women that struggle to leave and many that struggle to stay.

I am hoping my leaving acts as a sense of role modelling for my daughters. To role model that one deserves to be treated with kindness. I hope they at least have some idea or have received a message that one deserves to be treated well and to be happy in a relationship. Currently both speak of the hope to be married one day. It is my hope should they chose to do so that they hold out for a partner that is worthy of them and I wish the same for their partners.

As of this writing one of my daughters is engaged and I am very happy for them.

Chapter 16 Self-Reflection Questions:

* Are you willing to learn and practice HALT?

* How might this also be applied to your children?

* What ways do you self-care?

* Are you aware that self-caring is a way to lengthen your "fuse" so to speak, so you are less likely to blow up or explode?

* I used to wish we spent more time and resources on dates and building our relationship. I think we used to say dating was expensive. It does not have to be. I think the cost of building a relationship is an investment into a relationship.

* What are you doing to invest in your relationship?

* The saying goes if "mom and dad" are happy the children are more likely to be.

CHAPTER 17

Sex/Intimacy – Some Thoughts

Well I fear some of the things I have shared and will share in this book might cause me to lose some friends and loved ones, and also might bring judgement from others. I am trying to be true to myself and not be disrespectful of others. Since I want to write this book I think this chapter will be pertinent and hopefully helpful to some.

It seems to be getting easier to live with divorce. I still have times that I struggle and where I miss the familiar. But just because it is familiar does not always mean it was good. When I teach clients about Relapse and Recovery we used a metaphor of Recovery being like going up a down escalator. That if one stands still they will go back down. If you've ever gone up a down escalator one must keep moving and not remain at a standstill. Recovery requires action and not just thought or words.

Another metaphor about recovery is to compare recovery to the coziness of an old bathrobe, or other clothing item that is worn in and so comfortable. We may want to hold on to the familiar even if it is not necessarily functional any more. I had a favourite pair of boots and I really loved them, and they were so comfortable. Over time the boots did not look as good as they were worn out and the tips of the boots were damaged and the bottoms were wearing thin. I took the boots to one shoe maker and they did a terrible job and I paid when really I should not have (see Chapter 25 on assertiveness) as they had agreed to put a metal tip on and had not. So unsatisfied I took them to a second shoe maker and he was sweet but the shoes despite his best effort still looked awful and again more money was spent that could have gone into a new pair. This analogy suits me as to why I might stay stuck or not move up the escalator, as I did not want to let go of my comfortable but worn boots. Even after I replaced them I kept them in the back of my closet for a while. Sometimes it is hard to let go. I am not comparing an ex to an old pair of boots. Rather that sometimes we hold on to things that no longer are a good fit. Recovery is work and change. Not that people want to stay sick, stuck or unhappy they might be comfortable with what they know. The good news is that after change and living in a new way this too can become comfortable once again. Many of my addicted clients when first in recovery find it very difficult and after time sobriety can become their new comfortable norm.

In terms of my leaving my marriage and this chapter's topic of Sex and Intimacy- in terms of my marriage and our sexual relationship there were no complaints and comfort was there as we had been together for 25 years and knew each other intimately from a young age.

I was raised in a home where sex was not talked about, my mom did her best and read from a fact of life book (where there were blank spaces to insert the child's name while she read it to us, I think this was in effort to make the book more personal). It was not very informative, I believe I still have the little booklet. As far as my sexual development went I was shown menstrual pads and a belt (which was used at that time), but I don't recall being told what they would be used for. At least I had that much knowledge and managed to put 2 and 2 together when I had my first menses.

I had a wonderful grade 5-6 teacher that had a book of questions for the class on sexuality and she left this book on her desk and encouraged the class to borrow it. The main thing I remember from that book was that if a boy states that you, "must relieve his erection or says that it is painful", do not believe him and it is not the girl's responsibility. That I think was helpful education. I went to a Catholic High School and the sex education was awful. The teachers spoke of sex being horrible and the class was, I believe, trying to instill fear of STD (Sexual Transmitted Diseases) including videos. The double message was that sex is horrible and yet to save sex for the blessing of marriage. Fortunately, I was able to work out a lot of that confusion before getting married.

Being single again had me looking at all these damaging messages including some other newer messages. The new rules seemed to be about how it is good to sleep with everyone and yet to not commit (largely seen on social media, in movies and on TV). Other divorce books have written about this.

Singleness is an individual's journey pardon the pun. What may work for one may not work for another. I have discovered that I like to be in a monogamous relationship. I had a roommate that stated that for her, one-night stands are wonderful. I also noticed that under a year she was in a committed relationship.

I have not had many experiences to speak of.

So... Divorced/Separated people here are some things I have learned.... You can have great sex with not the nicest of people. You can have sex that is not that great with some wonderful people. One fella I really thought I was in to was so dishonest and fortunately I was able to figure this out within a few weeks of our dating after having known him for several months on-line. I was angry at myself for not seeing it sooner. One of my friends complimented me by saying I figured it out within two weeks and she thought that was great. I didn't want to have such harsh lessons.

Another guy even lied to me, a doctor none the less. I told him it's not ok and that it just confirms that I should listen to and trust my gut. He had been a very jealous man. I have a theory that jealous ones are likely the cheaters and they are suspicious because cheating is what they do.

I had a friend that remarried and after their engagement her fiancé cheated on her and she never discovered until after they were married. Her husband had no intention of telling her. She found out because a woman he cheated with had called their number to state that the woman calling had a STD. It turned out that because the woman caller spoke with my friend and found out that my friend was his wife that had answered the phone, the caller thought under the circumstances that the wife deserved to know.

As a high school student in a sex education class the teacher (a man) shared that sex is like having a good bowel movement. This was prior to any sexual experience and I thought quite a rude analogy.

We were taught of the dangers and not of the respect afforded a relationship and waiting until you felt cherished. I have taught some Respect Ed classes in high school and the material I used was more concerned about relationships. Respect and how you treat people and wish to be treated is still sound advice when one is looking for friends or lover(s). In teaching youth I like to emphasize if someone cares about you they will wait until you are ready and not pressure you, this is good advice for adults too.

Joy Blossom, BA(Adv)Psy, C.Hyp

Chapter 17 Self-Reflection Questions:

*   What are some of the things you learned about sex and intimacy while you were growing up?

*   Do you need to re-evaluate these lessons?

*   In society we still have double standards: For example, if a man is to have multiple partners he is then often called a "stud". Whereas if a woman has more than one partner she is often labeled a "slut".

*   If you wish to explore other types of relationships you might wish to read about alternative relationship styles. This does not mean this is right for you it may just give you an awareness of what some other couples do.

        A good book on Polyamory is: The Ethical Slut: A practical Guide to Polyamory, Open Relationships;

        Authors include: David Crosby; Dossie Easton, Catherine A. Liszt; Janet Hardy.

*   Do you have someone safe to explore sexual ideas with? This could just be conversation.

*   What constitutes a healthy relationship for you?

Getting Easier

It seems to be getting easier for me to live with divorce. I have been convincing myself that I deserve someone who is "into me". My ex did not seem to be that "in to me" and his judgement was harsh and yet I tried to give him many benefits of the doubt – recognizing that his judgment might be due to his being tired. He told me after the divorce that I never forced him to change (true I knew I could not change another). In his mind if I had fought more he thinks he might have changed. It was as if he said because I had compassion this allowed him to continue misbehaving. I thought being kind would lead him to desire to change – no pressure. I will not accept him blaming my kindness as his seeing it as a green light for bad behaviour. I can't believe he blamed me for his bad behaviour. I refuse to accept any part of that. I believe I would try to do better if someone is compassionate with me. Anger is not my preferred way to be motivated.

In sports my ex excelled with coaches that were mean and angry. I always excelled in sports when people had fun and were good sports.

My current boyfriend is patient, tolerant and kind. I am, though I had my walls up off and on, appearing to do much better in this relationship, I feel safer. I am realizing, just like I did in my marriage that others don't make me happy, this is my job. Others can make it easier to be around, less tense, so easier for me to enjoy them and life.

My boyfriend was away this weekend with scuba diving. I have tried to line up some social activities, most have not worked out. Instead I found myself baking, walking and spending some time with my youngest. Tomorrow will be my social day. As an adult I have always been fine with alone time. As a child I did not always like to have alone time. As a child (before cell phones) I would go through my own hand written phone book and call friends until I found someone to play with. My ability to thrive in alone time as an adult probably helped me to last in a marriage longer and is helpful now that I am out on my own. Independence is a good thing. I think one reason I left is -yes I can be alone- but I like a relationship.

Another thing I wonder is if my ex and I had continued our daily walks would we have drifted so far apart? I walked today before writing this down. I enjoy walking alone; yet, I think walking with a partner or friend brings closeness, a chance to catch up and to bond.

One of my clients shared that when you drive a car you only quickly glance into the rear-view mirror but otherwise you focus ahead. This is what I have found the most effective in moving forward. I live in the moment more and will have some idea where I am going but for now I am in the present.

In my work things can change in an instant. For example, I may have clients booked then I may get called for trauma work so then my whole day changes. I clear my schedule, so I can do what needs to be done. Life can be like this. Being flexible is good for mind, body and spirit.

Chapter 18 Self-Reflective Questions:

* What are some things you can do to help you to live in the present? Describe them, make a list.

* Mindfulness is a key word in the world today. Perhaps you would be interested in exploring what it means and how to implement the concept into your day.

* What do you think of the saying - "time heals".

* Some views on meditation are that it is good to meditate 15 minutes a day and if you don't have 15 minutes you need to meditate for 30. Meaning when life is too busy that is when we really need to take time to slow down.

* There are many ways to live in the present. Even spending a few minutes outdoors can have the benefits of a meditaion. One way to tell if you have been mindful is if you actually see things on your walk, notice the color of the grass etc. At times we are not even aware of how we drove home it is just automatic.

* I find for myself I need to ground myself such as by noticing my feet on the earth. This is helpful as many times I am all in my head and that's ok too, but to accomplish tasks we also need to be in our body. What ways can you ground yourself?

* Being in your imagination can be a good thing too. In what ways are you creative?

CHAPTER 19

Sensitivity toward your Children as you embark on a new Sexual/Partner Relationship

I am not the expert in this, but I have decided it is worth mentioning in a book that has the title "Everything". I am a counsellor and have been counselling 35 years at this point. When clients get enamored in a new relationship after a divorce they may forget to consider the children. Children are adjusting too, no matter what the ages. I myself made the mistake of introducing my children too soon to a new boyfriend. I regret this, and I hope I have learned to do better. I hope you can learn from my sharing that you can avoid making the same mistakes.

I never had this person (that I introduced too soon to my children) overnight when I had my children.

I still caused more harm, I believe, by introducing them too soon. This may be part of the reason why my children did not like this individual and it was likely due to more than that.

I think by my children meeting this man too soon it further confused my children as they did not seem to admit to knowing that their father and I were having difficulties.

I had a teenage client whose mother would have sleepovers with her new partner and this teen shared how disgusted and hurt she was that her mother was having sexual encounters (including the bathroom) when the teen was able to hear. I have no idea if this woman knew she was not being considerate of her teenage child. At times I am not working with parents when I am working with a child/teen, plus there is confidentiality.

Our youngest was staying at her dad's one week to care for the dog. Her dad and his girlfriend asked if she could stay with me. They were going on a trip and their flight was leaving early and so they planned to stay at his place as it is closer to the airport. Out of consideration for our daughter they wanted to be respectful and not have her be there. My ex had texted me and stated his girlfriend was not comfortable with our daughter being home at the time. I texted my ex, "good on her", complimenting his girlfriend for her consideration.

This may not apply to all situations, my point is rather to consider the child/children, as sometimes as adults we think we have all of the rights. I want our daughter(s) to feel comfortable in their own home(s).

In my current relationship we have been together now for 5 years. We are considering living together, this has been a process that has included mostly my youngest daughter as she still lives at home.

One sad memory was that when I was dating my first boyfriend after our separation I brought him home for supper and he brought his daughter to join us, my daughter did not wish to join us at the table. I allowed her to eat in her room. Later when she came out she had such hurt in her eyes as she saw this other girl about her own age sitting at her spot at the table. I share this story just to bring awareness.

This same daughter never liked anyone I dated, and she has "good guts" (judgement) and I have learned to respect that. The current fellow I am with she would initially sometimes be rude and tell him it was time to leave. Her insults for him to me directly were very mild so I suspected she might like this one. About a year later when she had grown to like him I asked what had happened? She shared she had just been protecting my heart. I thanked her and reminded her that this is my job. She is of the dating age now and I too feel protective. Just remember if a child or teen is upset it may have something to do with their fears for themselves and or for you the parent. My boyfriend and I sometimes look back and see how far we have come in our comfort with each other and with our children and dating. They are all now young adults.

I know I have guilt as I never imagined getting a divorce. I believe it has been hard on all of us. I would rather try to accommodate them as I have made some huge mistakes initially. Granted I was hurting and confused.

My oldest seems more comfortable with my current boyfriend and wonders why we do not live together, and she sometimes blames this on my youngest. I have told her that we have not yet moved in together not because of her younger sister but rather more because I am not yet ready. I do want my youngest to feel comfortable in her own home. She still has another 2 years of University where I expect she will call my home her home, so I want her included in this decision.

A few exceptions initially about spending the night had been made. For example, one weekend we, my boyfriend, my daughter and other friends went to the lake. There were enough separate rooms, but because it was a holiday I asked my daughter prior to going if she would be ok if I shared a room with my boyfriend and I believed her when she responded she would be ok with this.

Another time was for the Christmas Eve the last two years my boyfriend stayed the night, so he did not have to wake up on Christmas morning alone.

Up Down and Sideways

It blows my mind how up, down and sideways I am. Watching my daughters (then 17 and 20) struggle with their own relationships made me wonder if being single was the way to go. My current relationship seems really awesome and yet I have the ability to pick it apart. My youngest had her first heart break and watching her hurt was awful. My oldest daughter's boyfriend suffered a family death– so of course he was hurting and at times his upset came out in their relationship. This too was hard to watch.

And yet here I am wondering about a second marriage. I awoke from a dream and in the dream, I went on a trip with my current boyfriend and ended up back with my ex-husband. I still love him my ex – yet I realize he did not put the effort into our relationship. And here I am with a fella that appears to be putting in effort and I struggle…WTF?!

So how many years, months and days does it take to get over someone?

How many years, months and days does it take to let someone in?

I've toyed with the idea of getting remarried. It appears there are pros and cons. We have talked about getting married when I initially wrote this I was more leaning towards the benefits of not getting married. I love freedom! I am a night owl and my two main love relationships in my life, have been early birds. The first was not very understanding that this was not about him, it was more of who I am. I often get a "second wind" (energy) around 10 pm. My current boyfriend tries to be accommodating yet I wonder at times if he judges me for it. Living on my own I can have my own sleep routine and much more freedom to do as I please. I resented in my marriage how I was expected to provide the cooked meals the majority of the time. Yet when married we spent a year in Japan and we worked for the same company teaching in different cities and living in another. I was expected to work later and my ex (husband at the time), appeared fine with cooking the majority of meals then. I love to bake not a huge fan of cooking meals.

Sure, some nights I would like my boyfriend to stay, other nights I am just fine kissing him good night knowing I will see him the next day or soon.

Prior to my daughter having her own boyfriend she didn't really like my boyfriend being here. Once she had a boyfriend she was busy with her boyfriend and seemed more accepting when mine was over.

Now that she is single again I think she sometimes "gives off the vibe" that she wishes it was just us again. For example, my boyfriend and I went out for supper and my daughter said she was so hurt. She stated we don't see each other as much and asked me why wouldn't we share supper together? I reminded her when I do cook she usually eats, thanks me and heads to her room. I do try to make myself available to her. We do invite her at times to join us when we go out to eat and for sure if we are cooking at home. I've also reminded her she is an adult now and I no longer feel obliged to do the cooking.

Navigating love relationships, with your partner and with your children, teens and young adult children can take some awareness and my intent is to try to be kind and also to self-care. My mother and perhaps her generation were, it appears to me, to be taught not to think of herself before others. I like the saying, "If mama ain't happy then nobody is happy." Of course, this can be taken out of context, but to me my own needs are a part of the equation.

One man I dated did not respect when I said I did not want him to meet my children as yet. He stalled and would not leave as he knew my daughter would be home soon. I would "shoo" him out the door and he would try to linger to meet my daughter. He even gifted her a Birthday present. I did not continue to date this man as he was not respectful of my wishes. I also saw this as disrespecting my child.

Being treated with kindness and in a respectful manner is very important to me. I may indeed decide to remarry. My best friend died a couple of years ago and she and her new husband sat me down prior to her death to insist on my having a prenuptial arrangement. I have had clients that even though they had a prenuptial agreement it was not upheld by the law due to moving provinces. Honestly, I have not yet checked into this. The same girlfriend had a postnuptial agreement as things had changed with property after their marriage. This was extremely important to her. I believe my current partner is a fair man and we could, if we would marry and then separate/divorce be fair. I guess one never knows.

I would say right now my main reason to hesitate on the "living together" part is due to my desire for freedom. I am however a bit of a romantic and do like the idea of a marriage. If any of you reading this care to share some viewpoints, please let me know.

Chapter 20 Self-Reflective Questions:

* What would a marriage after divorce mean to you?

* Do you see yourself living with another partner?

* Would you live in your house, their house or would you start by purchasing or renting a place together?

* What would your children think?

* Would everyone have a room or would some need to share?

* Who would parent whom?

* Are you informed about prenuptial agreements? Do they hold up if you move Provinces, States or Countries?

* How long does living together constitute a Common Law Marriage? Are you aware once considered common law the law may see each of you as having certain rights in regard to your property and the property of your partner?

* Is marriage different than a committed relationship? If so how?

CHAPTER 21

Blurred Lines

Another incident early on in my realizing I needed to leave was in the following song:

The song is called "Stuttering", by Fefe Dobson. The following lines had meaning for me that made me feel I must tell my then husband that I was being dishonest with myself and with him:

"If you can't be honest with me
Then I'm afraid this is the end.

Hurry up, hurry up.
If you ever really cared about me.
Tell the truth, give it up…."

Listening to this song made me feel I must tell my then husband that I was interested in someone else. I had not met this man until after my then husband and I had already had a divorce conversation. We were already in trouble. But this song reminded me of my loyalty to my husband and I told him I had feelings for another and he was already aware of this. I have previously written about his tying his shoe and asking me or stating that his friends wondered if there was another man. I had responded I have a man friend and at that point it was not more.

This man gave me positive regard or attention that my own husband had not been giving. I do think if my own "Needs" had been met in my marriage and I don't mean sex but rather intimacy I would not have been likely to be attracted outside of my marriage.

I have many clients that have "emotional" and sometimes "sexual" relationships outside their marriage often because their own needs are not provided. I witness with clients that their affair or affairs are often not "real" as in they may just have the enchantment of an early relationship without actually knowing or seeing who they are having the affair with. They may not see the person they are having an affair with as a real person, "warts and all". Some meet their "affairs" in away places and may have no idea of who they are with. They may see this other person in their own community but only meet in a hotel and not in the "real world". You may not have the non-romantic parts in this type of a relationship, such as paying the bills, caring for children or whatever real life responsibilities there are. In my case this other person seemed to like me, was attracted to me and treated me with attention, yet I truly did not know this person. Some affairs are so not based in reality.

Having left my husband without a break of just the two of us - blurred my grief, of our relationship having ended. Perhaps this is why it is taking me so long to let go.

In the book, Rebuilding – When Your Relationship Ends, by Bruce Fisher, EdD and Robert Alberti, PhD. The authors speak of when your first relationship after your divorce ends it can bring you back to grieving your original partner / your divorce. This was the case for me.

My ex and I never seemed to have a clear break, we both seemed to cloud our relationship after it was over by one if not both of us being involved with others. I will never know if having others helped us in ending our relationship or if it just made it messier.

Chapter 21 Self-Reflective Questions:

*   If you are planning on leaving your love relationship what do you need to do prior to doing so?

*   Have you tried to let your partner know that you are not happy in your current relationship?

*   Is there someone you are interested in? Can you put that interest on hold while you leave the relationship you are in?

*   Have you made an appointment to see a lawyer to find out what your rights are?

*   Do you have support in place while you work toward separation?

CHAPTER 22

Grad(s)

We have celebrated two grade 12 graduations since our divorce. The first one I do not think I had a boyfriend. My ex had broken up with his girlfriend at the time of our first daughter's grad. Just a note he had dated a mother of our oldest daughter's friend and in retrospect this was very hard on our daughter when they split. It appeared out of loyalty to her mother my daughter lost a good friend.

For the first grad we did not have partners or dates to consider in planning our oldest daughter's grad.

We were amicable so were able to sit at the ceremony and at the banquet together. It was still a hard day to be together and yet I think we were both grateful that we could share in this special day together. I stayed later at the dance to watch and to keep the change of clothes for when our daughter changed out of her gown, so I could take the gown after the dance. I was at the dance alone. I remember thinking it could have been fun to dance as my ex and I had always enjoyed dancing together.

I guess the highlight and yet it was difficult was earlier in the day we had met as a family to have professional pictures taken. I was glad to have some family pictures including both parents for our daughter and some also with all of us. One of my favorites was taken at the top of a train bridge.

For the grad of our youngest daughter we each had

our own partners or dates. My youngest I had asked if it would be easier for her if no partners came to the banquet, and she agreed this would be easier. Both partners were allowed to come to the ceremony, my ex's partner did not come.

For family pictures earlier in the day I had asked our daughter if she wanted both her dad and I in the pictures. She responded that she did. When speaking with her dad I told him her wishes wondering if he felt the same?

His response was, "We are family – people don't spend as long as we are together and not consider themselves family."

I was and am so grateful for this response. I am sure some divorced people would not agree, but I felt so grateful.

My daughters have complimented us on our ability to get along. They may not always like us in the same room, I say this because of some comments one of my daughters has shared with me. Another comment I have possibly already shared is that she can't get away with getting in trouble like some of her friends from divorced families because her dad and I talk. In other sharing she expressed that some parents don't know what their teens are up to because of the lack of communication between parents. I am aware this can happen in families where parents are together. I took this as a compliment.

I give kudo's to my ex for scouting out a lovely location for photos for our youngest daughter's grad and that some of these included the entire family. We decided not to invite either of our new partners to the photo session. In these photo's my oldest had a boyfriend that took part in the family photos. It was nice to see some of just our daughters. They have been through a lot with our divorce and they have grown to be lovely young women. If someone asked if the children were impacted by our divorce I would say absolutely, yet fortunately they are resilient and we as a family are always growing. I think both of our daughters have the intent to one day get married. This leads me to believe they have not been totally disillusioned by marriage or coupledom.

For our youngest grad the banquet was lovely and she even said "grace" for the meal. For the dance I was the only one that stayed again being ready with a change of clothes for my daughter. The gift in this dance was that I was invited to dance with my daughter and her best friend and her best friend's family, so it was a treat.

In retrospect I am so grateful we were able to celebrate grad as a family. The next day I had planned to have a few people over to celebrate her graduation. Her father also planned to have a few people over. It ended up many were out of town, so he asked if I could have his guests over to my place, namely his brother and sister in law. I was happy to do this. Her father (my ex) did not join us. We had some guests for supper and others for a celebratory graduation cake. In writing this my best friend has since passed away and I believe this was the last time she could join us at my home. By then she was wheel chair bound and we quickly mowed the lawn and had cake outside, so she could join us. I am so fortunate that she could celebrate with us that day as she has been a huge support in our daughter's lives.

I'm trying to think if there is anything else about grad that I might mention. Costs of grad were shared. I believe her father paid for the banquet and I paid for photos. I am sure each family can work this out. I have seen some families that have not helped each other out in terms of expenses. I've even known some that will quit their job so as not to have to contribute to child costs, and I have even know of one case where a parent hid a large portion of his income to not pay child benefits. This would be harming your children and role modelling negative behaviour.

If grad is too expensive for a low-income family, there are some organizations that provide gently used gowns.

Divorced people can celebrate milestones of their children together. Though some may prefer to have separate celebrations. We have done both.

Chapter 22 Self-Reflective Questions:

* Do you have any family milestones or potential celebrations coming up?

* What are they?

* Is this something you wish to include your child(ren)'s parent in?

* Is your child in favor of having you both at the celebration? Will there be pictures involved? If so who do you see being in these pictures?

* Are there costs involved and how do you wish to approach these? Can some of these be a shared expense?

* What about seating arrangements?

* Are tickets needing to be purchased? Is there a limit to the number of tickets allowed?

* What about any respective partners of the parents? Do you wish to include them? What about if they have children, should they also be included? What about any other extended family?

CHAPTER 23

Christmas and blending families:

I invited my ex for one Christmas when I found out he and his girlfriend broke up as I knew from experience how it "sucked" to be alone at Christmas. It was a tentative invite as I was uncertain if they would get back together. I did not want him there in the morning as I found that was too hard on me Christmases prior as it was too much a reminder of being married. My boyfriend and I do not live together and he stated he would not wish to be there in the morning if my ex was there, but that he would be alright if he came for supper.

I told my ex that we would be eating a bit later as my boyfriend wanted to go to his son's as his son was hosting Christmas in the afternoon, so we would eat later to spread the meals out for my boyfriend.

I told my ex he could come earlier if he wished. When he arrived he was surprised I was home. I guess he thought I was with my boyfriend. I could have gone with my boyfriend, but I wanted to spend more time with my daughters as one was home briefly visiting from out of province.

Their dad exchanged gifts with our daughters and daughter's boyfriend. I did not have a gift for my ex – remember "the tea incident". He brought me a gift. Ironically, he had found a gift card his mom had given him and used it to purchase a book for me, "The Alchemist", an anniversary edition by Paulo Coelho. A book I had read and enjoy. Another surprise as years ago I do not believe he would like such a book and now he was inspired by it. People can change and interests can change.

We had a nice afternoon visit, I busied myself cooking while the others visited. My boyfriend later joined us for dinner. I believe we all had a nice time and a delicious meal. It was interesting as one of my daughters later voiced how she felt weird having her dad in our home. I hadn't noticed. And my boyfriend remarked something similar finding it odd that my ex appeared so at home even though he had never lived here.

As far as spending time with my boyfriend's family I did not want to be spending time with his ex. He accepted at first my turning down holiday invites with his immediate family (his ex and his two sons one of their partners and one partners parent and his ex's plus one). I still have mixed feelings on this, yet my boyfriend reminds me this is not about me and rather is about getting to know his sons and daughter in law.

I have found it difficult and yet doable and it has given me extra opportunity to get to know his children. On one occasion I invited my daughter to his immediate family Christmas dinner as otherwise it would have been just my one daughter and I that I would have cooked for. I thought things had gone relatively well. I am learning that I may not have an accurate read on other's feelings. It turns out my daughter had found it a difficult time.

The following year I had invited this same daughter to my boyfriend's extended family Christmas dinner. I had felt my daughter would like this as this family had the same German Mennonite traditions as my ex's family. My boyfriend had thought so many people would be too overwhelming for her.

As it turns out my daughter fit right in and even told me so. The food, the Christmas caroling and so many that were teachers put her at ease. My daughter is in Education studying to be a teacher. She even met a young teacher and they were both in Education and they had a good visit.

My boyfriend has also visited my extended families. He has stated he feels somewhat overshadowed by my ex as others were of course more familiar with my ex as we had been together 25 years. There are those that are making an effort to get to know my boyfriend and others that do not seem interested.

In my family of origin (the family I was raised in) I only have one brother as both of my parents are deceased. My brother has been very welcoming to my boyfriend and notices the caring way my boyfriend is to me. My brother is also divorced and though his divorce and mine are quite different he does seem to have a good understanding of how a divorce can impact a person. My brother and I are close even though we live in different provinces, we talk a lot on the phone and try to keep each other updated on what things are going on in each other's lives. My brother has a son that I make effort towards. Their relationship is complicated also because of divorce.

My boyfriend has also met my birth mother, who I refer to as my BOM (Birth Mom). I find it weird that her (my BOM) second husband and my current boyfriend share the same first name.

As far as extended family for my family of origin it appears my cousins are open to getting to know my boyfriend though again we live in different provinces so actual time together is limited.

I do wish my parents had met my boyfriend and my children, but this was not the case. Though I do believe spiritually they have.

This past Christmas my youngest daughter spent a lot of time with my ex and his new partner as his girlfriend has adult daughters and my daughter stated this was a factor. They did things we normally would do together such as build a gingerbread house, though they made theirs out of chocolate. I know this as my daughter wanted me to help her buy the decorative candy. I tried to not be jealous and tried to see this as a natural progression of my ex's new relationship. I think this current partner for my ex is likely to be long lasting. I never had this feeling about the others. This year neither of us, my ex or I made any effort to include each other with our children at Christmas. I am not sure what this will look like if grandchildren are involved.

Relationships are often more complex than we might think. Relationships will change as time goes on and as new circumstances arise. It is my hope that as a divorced couple we can adjust and be a part of our daughters' lives.

Chapter 23 Self-Reflective Questions:

* Do you believe it is in the best interest of the children (adult children count too) to celebrate the holidays together?

* Is this something you might like to try?

* Do you want to ask the other participants (children/ new relationship) what their views might be about this?

* Is it better to let the children go to both places and not join together with both parents? Is there some benefit to having all parties involved somehow?

* Can you put some boundaries in place prior to the different occasions?

* Is it ok to self-care and not have the other parent involved if you believe it is too difficult for you?

* How might it work with extended family?

* Do you want to invite your children to your new relationship's extended family?

* Would a pro/con list help in your decision?

CHAPTER 24

My Best Friend's Funeral

My best friend died, and I am happy to say I was with her and her family as she passed away peacefully after a three year battle with ALS also known as Lou Gehrig's Disease. ALS is a disease that gradually paralyzes people because the brain is no longer able to communicate with the muscles of the body that are typically able to move at will. Someone with ALS will lose the ability to walk, talk, eat, swallow and eventually breathe. There is no cure and few treatment options at the time of this writing.

Since we were so close I was invited by the family to give the eulogy at the funeral. My friend has been an important person in my life for years. My daughters were also very close to her. My ex knew how important this friend has been to me and knew her children as well. He let me know he would like to attend the funeral. This was the first time someone not related to him and that was a part of our lives had died since our divorce and that he would join us (my daughter and I and my boyfriend) at a funeral. I sat with my deceased friend's husband and her family. It was kind of new for me to see both my ex and my boyfriend and daughter sitting together.

I was grateful that my ex attended and I am thinking our daughter also appreciated his support at this time. He also texted me after complementing me on my eulogy which I also appreciated.

Joy Blossom, BA(Adv)Psy, C.Hyp

Oddly enough I ran into the ex-friends that had treated me poorly and slammed my daughters which ended my friendship with this couple. It likely was a time to forgive; however, I chose to maintain my integrity by being courteous and in addition I chose to not reignite this relationship. After I wondered if this was the "right" thing to do. I feel it is and that I maintained a boundary and choose not to have hurtful people in my life. I know forgiveness is good for me in the sense I can stop the poison from further hurting me. Forgiveness does not mean continuing in a toxic relationship.

Since the funeral I maintain a relationship with my deceased friend's husband. Gradually he no longer replied to my texts. I guessed that perhaps he is dating and being in contact with me, his past wife's best friend would be hard for him. We have recently been in touch again. My boyfriend ran into him and he was with a new woman. He introduced her to my boyfriend and noted please say hello to Joy for me. My boyfriend doesn't recall her name. I usually borrow this man's rototiller so will be seeing him once again this gardening season.

When someone dies, much like a divorce, sometimes those relationships with the loved ones that survived, may change.

Chapter 24 Self-Reflective Questions:

*   Can you support an ex when their loved one dies?

*   Feel free to revisit Chapter 6.

*   There is no right or wrong way to deal with or cope with a divorce. There are many pathways, the key is to try and maintain some common decency and integrity in my opinion. Are you able to know what common courtesy is in regard to an ex? If so what might this look like?

*   Relationships end in other ways than divorce. Are you able to self-care when other losses occur?

*   What are some ways that you can self-care at a difficult loss?

*   Loss can be cumulative; one loss might trigger another loss, divorce can trigger other relationship losses. Please be aware of this. Where can you find support at difficult times in your life?

CHAPTER 25

Boundaries

In life and in divorce and even in marriage or any relationship, having boundaries, I believe is important. Somewhere I learned that we teach people how we wish to be treated. I know in my counselling life sometimes people are rude and even cruel, and this may have absolutely nothing to do with me personally. Some people are hurting and lash out and others might just be plain old mean.

My own mother allowed herself to be treated poorly by my father. This was partly due to his alcoholism. I wish she had been strong enough to stand up for herself. I still see people whether clients, strangers or friends that are mistreated. Heck, sometimes I allow others to treat me poorly. Anyone with teenagers has likely experienced this. As one of the developmental tasks is for teens to push away parents in order to be more independent. I often think of Dr. Seuss' character, the "push me pull me", a fictitious character that has a head at each end wanting to go in opposite directions. I have found adolescents will go back and forth from dependence - child self, to independence - adult self. Fortunately, creating healthy boundaries can help in relationships.

In university I had a class in communication and the professor did a good job in teaching the difference between: Assertive, Passive, Aggressive and Passive-Aggressive. I'm afraid I no longer remember who taught me the following, it might have been Dr. Sydia. The Passive-Aggressive image I came up with myself.

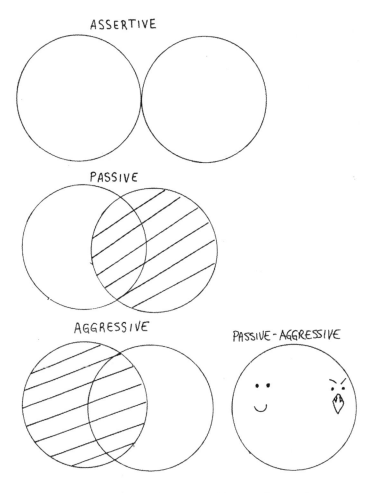

Assertive, Passive, Aggressive, Passive-Aggressive

Assertive:

Looks like two circles side by side, touching. Each circle represents each person's personal boundary. No one is challenging the other's boundary. Both are seen as equal.

Passive:

Looks like two circles overlapping where on the left is the passive person and on the right the shading shows where the boundary has been crossed by the other person. Sometimes the other person is not intending to cross boundaries it may be unintentional as no clear boundary was set.

Aggressive:

Looks like two circles overlapping but this time the shading is on the left circle and is overextending onto the circle on the right and this is usually intentional.

In aggression the aggressive person is stepping over the other person's boundary. When someone is acting aggressive, one can reply with assertive behavior. Aggression does not need to beget aggression.

Passive-Aggressive

Looks like one circle divided in half and the left side face is smiling and the right side is angry though is not seen and rather is hidden in the back. To the observer the anger is not apparent. The passive-aggressive person keeps their anger or feelings hidden from the observer. The passive-aggressive person often has the hidden intention to be harmful or aggressive.

I pride myself on mostly being Assertive as this is the ideal mode to communicate from. When being Assertive not only are you trying to respect other's rights while at the same time respecting your own. My default is likely to be passive. I also refer to it as "taking the bullet", where I will concede on my rights for the good of another. This can be also seen as "being a doormat" or as "egg shell walking". Being passive serves a purpose too. In one situation a client I worked with had been in an armed robbery and I believe his being passive in this particular situation saved his life.

Just like anything the more one practices the Assertive Communication style the more comfortable and natural it will be. The example I was given for each mode of communication was to imagine being seated in a classy restaurant. Once seated the view is of the men's bathroom. When the bathroom door is open one can see the urinal.

What would an Assertive person do?

An Assertive person would politely asked to move tables. And in most cases the server would be happy to oblige.

What might a Passive person do?

A Passive person would likely say nothing to the server but may under their breath voice a complaint and be negatively impacted by their seat location.

What might an Aggressive person do?

An Aggressive person would likely in an irritated, possibly in a loud rude manner, insist on being moved to another seat making a scene.

The Passive-Aggressive person would to your face appear fine but behind the scene they may lodge an attack or post a negative review.

Ideally it is likely best to deal with the situation in the moment and do so in an assertive manner.

It is still a choice and if one decides to not do anything (passive) and decides to still be civil this too can be a choice. To be assertive can take work. I remember once being at an out of town hockey tournament with my team mates and we went out for supper. Many of my team mates were drinking and perhaps the servers "assumed" all of the team were tipsy. My meal came to me burnt. I knew I could choose to ignore the condition of the food, but I chose to send it back politely explaining my issue with the food. We were staying in a hotel and food would not be available until the next day. Meanwhile I nibbled off other's plates and when the food did finally come, most had finished eating. I explained this to the server and suggested I receive a discount as the meat being burnt had not been my fault. Fortunately, the server "promoed" my meal, that is they gave it to me at no charge for the inconvenience. Being assertive does not always guarantee a positive outcome. It does however help one to remain kind.

I have at times taken bad behavior trying to give the other person the benefit of the doubt such as maybe they are tired etc. As I would prefer to have others do the same for me. Unfortunately, this approach has allowed others to take advantage of me which is not my intention. I would like to think if I give others the benefit of the doubt this kindness might have them appreciate the grace given and to act appropriately. Are you aware of which style you are likely to be?

Chapter 25 Self-Reflective Questions:

* Do I understand the differences of being Assertive, Passive, Aggressive and Passive-Aggressive?

* What is my preferred mode of these communication styles?

* Do I desire to try to be more Assertive? If so in what areas?

* What would I look like, sound like and act like, if I were being more assertive?

* Are there people in my life that are passive? What might I do or say with these people?

* Are there people in my life that are aggressive or passive-aggressive? Who are they? Is there something I can change in my own behaviour that might help me in these relationships?

***Please note: I must warn people if someone has controlled you in the past with words of aggression, at times, if you become more assertive these same people may get louder or more aggressive because they are surprised by the change. They may sense words no longer control you as in the past and may feel a need to physically lash out. It is called "upping the ante", which means being more aggressive in these interactions. They may try to get you to go back to being passive. It is important to add some safety measures if you are trying to learn to be assertive in these aggressive relationships.

CHAPTER 26

Moving Forward

I feel like I am becoming much more adjusted to being through a divorce. As I have mentioned my ex and I are able to celebrate events with our daughters together and even our losses. Right from the beginning we tried to be courteous and kind even though we did not always succeed. I am guessing it's a fair bet that we will still have bumps and bruises.

We have yet to navigate weddings or grandchildren. I have witnessed others in divorce who have done so and some without success. I am hopeful we will find a win-win way of doing so. I love the analogy that love is like fire not like pizza. One can run out of pizza, whereas love does not run out rather it expands and can burn bright and continue to grow. There can be enough love for everybody so to speak, it won't run out. I do not need to diminish my light for you to have your light. Just like flowers in a garden all can be beautiful.

I hope I can remember this as these stages come into my life or our lives.

If any of you as readers have found ways to overcome these hurdles and to do better as ex-husbands and ex-wives I would be happy to hear from you.

I still care about my ex and I still need to learn where we may need to consider each other and when it is none of my concern? For instance, this week was my Ex's Birthday and I was not sure if a Birthday wish was appropriate via text? Similarly, I am also now learning, having adult children, what part is of my concern and what is not? This is a process.

As far as my newer love relationship goes I still make steps forward and at times then fall back. I personally have a difficult time trusting and living just for today. I am fortunate to have many tools that can help me to navigate. My friend before she died, she and her husband (a second marriage) talked to me more about "Pre-nuptial agreements", something I may wish to do in the future. In each person's province or state there are rules about how long one can cohabitate before being considered to be in a legal common law (CL) relationship where property laws take effect. I am still not living with my current boyfriend, though I suspect this could change.

I still have one adult child at home, a university student and perhaps we will wait until she is ready to move out. I have heard pros and cons about a couple moving into his or her home and about selling both and purchasing a new home together. My best friend had kept her place after moving into her boyfriend's home as a safety net. Then when he sold his place they together moved into hers and then fortunately they were able to sell and purchase a different home together.

I love to travel so who knows where I or possibly we might end up. I might like to be a "snowbird", someone who keeps her home and travels to hot destinations in the winter. So many things to consider. I do not know how to predict the future so even the best laid plans may not be.

I thank all of you for going on this journey with me thus far. I hope some of my sharing will help you as you encounter yours.

Blessings,

Joy Blossom

Chapter 26 Self-Reflective Questions:

*   Are there any lessons you want to make note of for your own relationships?

    Please write in point form some of these points to refer to on your journey.

*   Are there questions remaining in navigating a divorce? Feel free to list these and send these to me. Is there anyone you know that has had to deal with the issue? Do you feel comfortable asking them what and how they managed the issue?

*   Remember we are all on a journey and what might work for me might not work for you. Sometimes when I hear how others have dealt with an issue it gives me an idea of how I might use their story to help me. Sometimes hearing others is a warning and helps me to avoid their mistakes. This is my hope as well that prevention and growth may help you to avoid mistakes I or others have made.

*   Do you think you are doing a good job navigating your divorce? If yes congratulations! If no congratulations as you are human or a soul having a human experience! Are there some things you can improve on or do different? Is there someone you can talk to that might help you find your way? This person can be a friend. There are also professionals that can assist

you. Remember it is your journey so find someone who you feel is a good fit to learn from, share with and to lend their encouragement while you navigate your way.

Thank you for letting me share my journey with you,

Blessings to you!

Joy Blossom

Printed in the United States
By Bookmasters